The Composer in the Market Place

"Lucky for you I can't tell what you're playing."

A cartoon from the Daily Mirror, *22 April 1965*

The Composer in the Market Place

ALAN PEACOCK & RONALD WEIR

WITH A PREFACE BY ASA BRIGGS

This will prove a brave kingdom to me,
Where I shall have my music for nothing.
SHAKESPEARE · THE TEMPEST · III · 2

FABER MUSIC

First published in 1975 by
Faber Music Limited
38 Russell Square, London WC1
© Alan Peacock and Ronald Weir 1975
ISBN 0 571 10011 2
Design and production by S & M Tucker
Printed and bound in Great Britain by
William Clowes & Sons, Limited
London, Beccles and Colchester

Preface

Many of the biggest social and cultural changes go unchronicled until they are succeeded in their turn by new changes. It is then usually that the historians take over from the prophets.

The period covered in this book – seventy years of history – has seen immense social and cultural changes which only now are beginning to be placed in perspective. They are comparable with and in some respects continuous from the great social and cultural changes of the industrial revolution. It was a twentieth-century musician, writing in 1935, not a factory worker writing in 1835, who exclaimed, 'the machines have seized us, devoured us, and cast us forth again in a thousand duplications'.

The Performing Right Society, an important institution which is little known outside professional and institutional circles, is celebrating its Diamond Jubilee. It was founded in 1914 just before the Great Divide of the twentieth century. Yet the social and cultural changes which have concerned it at every stage of its history can all be traced back to the period before 1914. What we now think of as 'electronic circuitry' had its origins in what both music publishers and musicians called then 'mechanical music'. It was then, as William Boosey put it, that it began to be recognized that 'eventually a composer's performing rights might be even more valuable than his publishing rights'.

Only after 1918, however, did the really big changes take place, and only since the 1950s have we been able to relate them all to each other – a new and still developing technology, applied to entertainment as much as to work; a new and changing public, influenced both by education and by market forces, some of them very powerful institutional forces within the market; a revolution in sensibilities and in the language as much as in the techniques of communication.

This book is essential reading for any one who wishes to trace the patterns of change. It draws upon the scattered work of others, work which leaves many gaps, but it also breaks much new ground. It rightly rejects technological determinism, pointing throughout its chapters to institutional influences, like the rise of the BBC or the advent of commercial television. Indeed, it states explicitly in its postscript that the major influences on the market for musical composition in the foreseeable future will be more of an institutional than a technical character. At the same time, it insists that since there are many different kinds of composers, performers and organisers, some profoundly sensitive to their 'public', some geared to the market, the study of the economics of musical composition must be concerned always both with institutions and with people.

Above all, this book is not just a chronicle, valuable though a chronicle is. Its approach is analytical, and it pioneers the application of economic theory – concepts and methods – to musical composition. It may well encourage further studies not only of related themes in the twentieth century – 'media studies' for example, or studies of the agency business, of fashion or of advertising – but of earlier centuries when the economics of musical composition were quite different. Music may sometimes serve, in Shaw's phrase, as the 'brandy of the damned': it has always served as the food of the living. The story of the attempts of composers to carve out a living for themselves through the centuries provides one of the links between economic and aesthetic and cultural history.

ASA BRIGGS

University of Sussex

Contents

Illustrations

Acknowledgements

We are very grateful indeed to the large number of composers, songwriters and publishers who provided us with valuable information about their economic and financial activities. We would have been glad to have mentioned them all individually, but as several have preferred to remain anonymous, we have respected their wishes by mentioning none of their profession by name, with one understandable exception. Much of the information about the economic circumstances of composers was derived from a survey of their earnings, and we owe a special debt to Sir Arthur Bliss, President of the Performing Right Society, for agreeing to canvass his fellow-composers by letter in order to help our enquiry.

This study is a by-product of a wider investigation commissioned by the Perfoming Right Society. The Society gave us extensive use of its many publications and considerable source material, and we are glad to record our thanks to its officials for extracting information from its files and for patient attention paid to our many queries. The Society's General Manager, Mr Michael Freegard, and its Legal Adviser, Mr Denis de Freitas, gave us generous helpings of their time, while our fellow-economist in the Society, Mr Marshall Lees, offered us valuable professional advice.

We have benefitted from having the friendly support of two of our York colleagues. Mr Christopher Storm-Clark, Lecturer in Economic and Social History, put his extensive knowledge of the social history of the inter-war period at our disposal and made a number of valuable suggestions which we have taken into account. Miss Janet Cubitt, Institute of Social and Economic Research, who acted as statistical assistant for the wider investigation, will observe that a few of the fruits of her work have been preserved in this volume.

Finally, we wish to thank Faber Music Ltd and particularly Professor Donald Mitchell for encouraging us to believe that the penetration of economics into the study of musical composition need not be wholly unwelcome.

Introduction

The main purpose of this study is to identify the influences on the supply of musical composition of all kinds in Britain in the course of the last seventy years. This has entailed a close examination not only of the ways in which composers, in association with publishers and others, have brought their creations before the public, but also of the legal and political environment which has become an increasingly important influence on the economic position of suppliers of music. The general approach, therefore, is historical and descriptive, but we have cast our study within a general framework which is derived from economic analysis. In doing so, we believe that we offer some new evidence to support well known propositions in economic analysis concerning the ways in which producers of goods and services, more particularly the professions, protect their interests in the face of uncertain market prospects.

In preparing this work we have encountered difficulties familiar to historians in collecting and weighing the evidence. Very little has been written before on this subject, and the amount of digging for new material has been considerable. We cannot claim to have completed a full prospecting operation, given the limited time at our disposal, and it may be that there are rich veins of documentary sources which remain undiscovered. We hope that we have at least whetted the appetite for more detailed studies of particular aspects of the market for musical composition, if only by revealing the compelling vigour and frankness with which musicians and their associates have stated their views on their economic position. Having concentrated on the study of the supply of musical composition, we have left open an opportunity to others to look more closely than we have at the structure of demand.

Statistical information about composers' incomes is largely lacking. However, it was possible, as this study was a by-product of a wider study of the present economic position of composers and publishers, to obtain by direct enquiry some information on the amount and composition of composers' earnings at a given date. This enabled us to give a broad indication of the composer's economic position at the terminal date of our historical survey (see tables in Chapter 1). Even then, the rather low response rate to our questionnaire and the analytical impossibility of applying what statisticians call 'confidence limits' to the information supplied means that we have only been able to make limited use of the data supplied. We nevertheless believe that the data assembled in Chapter 1 gives a fair impression of the earnings position of composers in 1971. Alongside the statistical survey, we were able to obtain useful information on the attitudes of composers and publishers to their market situation both by written statements and by personal interview.

I have been responsible for the planning of the work, including the economic analysis, for the identification and selection of a large part of the historical material and the statistical information on composers' earnings. But this is in every sense a joint work, and I must pay tribute to the skill and tenacity of my colleague, Ronald Weir, in historical detective work and in the conduct of interviews with publishers and others. He is mainly responsible for the drafting of the middle chapters of this work and for its historical perspective. I believe he has enjoyed our expedition into territory unfamiliar to the economist and economic historian as much as I have.

This work could not have been written without help from those closely connected with the musical profession. A full list of acknowledgments is given elsewhere, but we would like to record separately our special debt to Mr Royce Whale, formerly General Manager of the Performing Right Society Ltd.

He has played an important part in the economic history of musical composition in Britain, as readers of this volume will soon discover, and his own writings on his experiences and on the law of copyright provided invaluable source material. We are therefore doubly fortunate not only because we have had access to his published works but also because we have derived immense benefit from having to run the gauntlet of his many comments and criticisms. Several important suggestions put to us by him have been incorporated in the text. We are deeply grateful to him.

Alan Peacock

1
The Economic Characteristics of Musical Composition

Introduction

The study of any market for a commodity or service requires an analysis of the ways in which the forces of supply and demand interact in order to determine the terms on which property rights are exchanged. In any economy in which property rights are, by and large, in private hands, the consumer's enjoyment of a particular product requires him to give up part of his property by transforming it into cash which he exchanges for a title to a particular amount of the product or service in question. Over a long period of time, the terms of exchange may alter substantially and will depend on the techniques used in producing and marketing the product or service, the extent to which there is competition between sellers and/or buyers and changes in the tastes and preferences, and also the incomes (purchasing power) of buyers.

However distasteful it may appear to those who regard the creation of works of art as an activity which should be immune from the operation of market forces, the fact remains that rights in musical works have been bought and sold in the open market in the Western World at least since the Church ceased to be the dominant employer of musicians. Strangely enough, little study has been made of the market for musical composition, yet this is a market in which a large proportion of the population of this country enter at some stage in their lives, if only to buy a record as a Christmas present or a cinema seat in order to watch a film for which background music has been specially written.

This particular study covers a period in which striking changes took place in the market conditions for composition. One hundred years ago the taste for music was satisfied by public performance in concert hall or opera house, and by buying a 'home-kit' for performance in the form of a piano together with the additional purchase of music lessons. Today alternatives have been widened considerably by striking technological developments which have produced the radio, television, phonograph and, latterly, the audio and video cassette. Today, 'she shall have music wherever she goes', without the presence of a single musician. In essence, this study is the story of the impact of these technological changes on the economic position of the composer, publisher and, to a lesser extent, the executant musician.

Though the study of the evolution of the market for composition entails a historical approach, we found it useful in planning this work to impose a general framework on the narrative which has been derived from standard economic analysis. Thus we asked ourselves the following kinds of question:

Are there any particular characteristics of musical composition which distinguish it from other goods and services?

What features distinguish the terms on which composition can be sold from goods and services in other markets?

Are these features a function of the nature of composition itself, or the legal system, or of the competition (or lack of it) between buyers and sellers?

Given the market conditions for composition, are composers and publishers likely to behave in ways which accord with the usual predictions made by economists?

We believe it will give the reader a better understanding of the particular issues discussed in our economic history of the market for musical composition if we provide some general answers to these questions in advance of the historical narrative.

The 'Product'

There are three particular features of musical composition as a 'product' which distinguish it from most other goods and services and which vitally affect the demand for composers' creations and the other services, such as publishing and performing, which help to bring compositions before the listener.

Firstly, production consists essentially of performances of the composers' works, music being considered at one time as the prime example of a perishable service.[1] Our historical survey covers a period during which this characteristic of composition has virtually disappeared. Though live performances are still in demand and are perishable, in the sense that they cannot be stored for future use except as memories, it is now technically feasible for music to be stored on record and tape. In principle, it is possible to maintain the 'stock' of musical composition intact without the employment of a single additional musical performer. In the course of the period covered by our narrative, the possibility has not been fully realized, for two reasons:

The first is that the public is interested in new interpretations of familiar works on records, and that recorded music fails to arouse the sense of occasion which goes with performance. In addition, reproduction is continually improving and, although old recordings can be refurbished, new recordings seem to be preferable. The second reason is that since performing musicians have no property right in the reproduction of their skill by mechanical method, they have sought by other means to restrict the output of recorded music through the mass media.[2]

Nevertheless, the fact that performance can be 'stored' means that if composers claim a right in performance, their interest must extend far beyond the confines of the concert hall. The

1. Thus Adam Smith characterized musical performance as 'an activity which does not fix or realize itself in any permanent subject or vendible commodity which endures after the labour is past'. See *The Wealth of Nations*, 1776, Book 2, Chapter 3.
2. *A Report on Orchestral Resources in Great Britain*, 1970, Arts Council of Great Britain, 1970, p.48.

pursuit of this interest forms one of the most intriguing aspects of the development of the market for composition in the twentieth century, not only in Britain but throughout the world.

Fortunately, for some classes of composers and for performing musicians, additions to the stock of musical compositions are still in demand. In the case of 'pop' and, to some extent, of 'light' music, the stock of music is rendered rapidly obsolescent by changing musical taste. This may produce a conflict of interest between composers, for it means that new compositions gain income at the expense of older compositions still in copyright. What evidence there is on this subject suggests that the 'peak' of earnings of popular composers who are regularly engaged in producing compositions takes place in the earlier years of their working life, whereas the reverse is true in the case of 'serious' composers. For the serious composer, indeed, changing musical taste may not increase the demand for contemporary music relative to 'older' music but alter the relative popularity of composers whose works have long since been out of copyright. That competition between the dead and the living is a serious matter is evidenced by the fact that, at the terminal date of this study, works of British and foreign living composers, while comprising nearly 37 per cent of all works in the Royal Festival Hall programmes during the 1968–69 season, occupied less than 11 per cent of programme time.[1]

Secondly, whereas for most physical products those who wish to enjoy them must pay for them and their enjoyment precludes others from doing so, the same is not generally true of music. It is possible to exclude those not prepared to pay for listening to a concert in the Festival Hall, but the costs of excluding 'non-payers' rises very rapidly when it comes to certain forms of mechanical reproduction. Striking examples of this problem are found in the attempt to license transistor radios and would be

1. A recent graduate in Economics at the University of York, Miss Adele Fox, has written a short dissertation on the price and output policies of London orchestras which indicates by statistical analysis that the 'older' the composer, the greater his positive influence on box-office receipts, even allowing for the skill of the orchestra and the reputation of conductor and soloists.

found if it were decided to charge a fee for 'home-dubbing' of radio broadcasts of music. Furthermore, whether or not charging for performance is practicable, enjoyment of a broadcast performance, for example, by one person does not preclude enjoyment by another, for all those within reasonable listening range can benefit.

The third characteristic of music as a product is one to which this work devotes a good deal of attention. As the second characteristic suggests, there may be immense practical difficulties in deciding what constitutes 'performance' of music and in detecting whether or not 'performance' is taking place. However, before there can be an incentive for producers of music to seek ways of circumventing these difficulties, it must be accepted by society at large that the composer has a property right in both the publication and performance of music. To a considerable extent the history of the market for musical composition over the last seventy years is the history of the composers' battle to overcome persuasive attempts to restrict by law the right in his intellectual property, both in terms of the length of life of his copyright and the area of its operation. Thus, while no time limit is generally placed on the enjoyment of a return from physical (capital though transfers of such property may be taxed, e.g. at death), this is certainly not the case with intellectual property. The reasons for this difference cannot be explored at this stage, but the record of the debate over the determination of composers' rights, given in the following chapter, may throw some light on the differences in treatment.[1]

The Market Environment of the Composer

These three characteristics of the product entail that composers have to face particular difficulties in obtaining a return for their efforts, in addition to the normal risks of independent professional

1. For further discussion of the economic issues, see Alan Peacock, 'The Economic Value of Musical Composition', *Beiträge zu einer Theorie der Sozialpolitik* (eds. Kulp and Stützel), Berlin, 1973.

business. As we have observed, composers have encountered strong opposition to the acceptance of the principle that their property rights embrace performance as well as publication, and, even if performance has come to be accepted as part of these rights, the definition of performance is far from easy.

Even if these rights are clearly defined, their negotiation and enforcement could impose costs on the individual composer which in most cases would far outweigh the expected financial return. If property rights were confined only to the control over publication, piracy may be difficult to detect and, even if detected, it may be difficult to stamp out. In fact our history begins with the announcement of the Music Publishers Association in April 1905 that they would accept no more music for publication until the law afforded adequate protection against pirates who sold cheap lithographed reproductions without permission or payment. The problem of piracy still remains for millions of disc records are made and sold each year without payment to authors or composers of copyright works.[1]

But even if piracy can be stamped out, the large majority of composers are clearly not in a position to afford the costs of negotiating rights with all potential users and the costs of collecting the agreed payments. It is one thing for a trader to collect money over the counter for the purchase of a bar of soap, but another for a composer by his own efforts to collect a royalty representing the agreed return from a new work which is being enjoyed not only by those attending a public performance but also by thousands of viewers through an international television link-up. As explained in detail later, composers and publishers were not slow to devise means for overcoming the difficulties arising from the nature of the product, yet a striking feature of our historical narrative is the poor predictions of those closely associated with the music market concerning the impact of technological change. A possible reason for this was the complication introduced by the fact that the mass media most affected

1. See J. A. L. Sterling, 'Piracy of Records', *The Music Industry: Markets and Methods for the '70s*, New York, 1970.

by such change, notably radio and television, were restricted by law in the number of outlets. Composers, publishers and musical performers were faced with powerful buyers of their services and in the case of the B B C – the dominant influence in broadcasting until recent times – by a buyer not obliged to follow commercial practices in realizing its policy objectives. The reaction to this situation by the producers of music and the consequential development of the system by which rights are negotiated with the media provides a fascinating case study in market economics in which, to anticipate, the inevitable result has had to be state regulation of the terms on which bargains are arranged.

Reactions of Composers to the Market Environment

The unusual features of music as a product and the institutional peculiarities of its market must place obstacles in the way of composers who seek even modest commercial success. Faced with the risks attached to making a living, it is pertinent to enquire how far composers have followed the common methods for dealing with such risks which are found in many occupations. Our historical survey will offer ample illustration that they have, though not all protective measures adopted by composers have been equally important.

We can classify these measures into those which are taken by the composer on his own, those taken by the composers with others with a stake in composition and those taken by composers collectively.

1. *Individual Action*   A common method used to reduce risk is for a producer to *diversify* his output so that his financial returns do not depend on demand conditions in one particular market.

There is no doubt that diversification has been one of the principal ways in which the composer has protected his financial position in the face of the difficulties he would otherwise face in having to rely solely on earnings from composition. There is ample 'negative' information in our historical survey to indicate that composers could not make a living from composition alone, much of it derived from the evidence presented to the 1928 Copyright Royalty (Mechanical Musical Instruments) Inquiry, which confirms a feature of the composer's life which is also found among even the best known names in the history of music. Among 'serious' composers of the nineteenth century, it is rare to find a prominent composer who did not also rely upon his prowess as an executant. While musical activities such as performing, editing, conducting and teaching were common supplementary means of support for composers, there are some striking examples of diversification, ranging from the Russian composers Borodin, Cui and Rimsky-Korsakov who were respectively a professor of chemistry, army general and naval officer, to Charles Ives who made more than a comfortable living as an insurance broker. Whether the term 'diversification' should be extended to marrying a rich widow, as in the case of Debussy or stumbling on rich patrons, as in the case of Wagner, is a debatable point!

In an amusing account of 'How Composers Eat', the American composer, Virgil Thomson,[1] offers the following classification of income sources:

1. Non-Musical Jobs of Earned Income from Non-Musical Sources
2. Unearned Income from All Sources
    (*a*) Money from home
        (*x*) His own
        (*y*) His wife's
    (*b*) Other people's money
        (*x*) Personal patronage
            (i) Impersonal subsidy
            (ii) Commissions
        (*y*) Prizes
        (*z*) Doles
3. Other Men's Music, or selling the By-Products of his Musical Education
    (*a*) Execution
    (*b*) Organizing musical performances

1. Virgil Thomson, *The State of Music*, Second Edition (Revised), New York, 1962.

(c) Publishing and editing
(d) Pedagogy
(e) Lecturing
(f) Criticism and musical journalism
(g) The Appreciation-racket
4. The Just Rewards of his Labor
   (a) Royalties
      (x) From music published
      (y) From gramophone recordings
   (b) Performing-rights fees

Unfortunately, we cannot give any indication of the changing earnings pattern of composers over the period covered by our historical survey, but, within the limits which beset the statistical data (described in our Introduction), we have some evidence of the contemporary position.

Table 1.1 (Item 1) records the *median* earnings in 1971 of (mainly) British composer members of the Performing Right Society who participated in a survey carried out on behalf of the P R S by Economists Advisory Group during 1972.[1]

The average earnings of the composers participating in the survey (which is much higher than the median[2]) would give a misleading impression. This is because a very small percentage of composers obtain very high earnings. Indeed the dispersion of composers' earnings was very wide in each category ('popular', 'serious' and 'light'),[3] with roughly two-thirds of all composers

1. 2,873 composers were invited to participate and 1,084 (38%) responded by completing a questionnaire giving details of their earnings from musical composition and other sources. Of these 575 were analyzed representing a final response of 20 per cent incorporated into the table.
2. The median earnings figure is arrived at by arranging all the composers in a group of ascending order of income and by then selecting the income of the composer falling in the middle of the group. Unlike the average it is not distorted by the presence of a few very high or very low incomes in the group.
3. Categorization of music between 'serious', 'light' and 'popular' inevitably involves subjective judgments and there is a further complication in that many composers produce works which would fall into more than one of these broad categories. Composers were asked to specify the category into which their works mainly fell, and the grouping this produced was subjected to some further analysis by specialist staff at the P R S.

Table 1.1 *Amount and Composition of Composers' Earnings in the United Kingdom in 1971*

	All Composers	'Popular' Composers	'Serious' Composers	'Light' Composers
I *Median* Earnings				
(i) from musical composition	£357	£356	£185	£472
(ii) from all sources	£1,924	£1,976	£1,780	£1,965
II Sources of Earnings:				
1. Musical Composition				
(a) *Performing Right royalties*	20·7%	16·4%	23·7%	25·9%
(b) *Mechanical Right royalties*	5·1%	7·0%	0·9%	4·5%
(c) *Sheet music earnings*	1·8%	1·8%	3·6%	1·1%
(d) *Dramatic performance royalties (e.g. opera, musical shows, ballet)*	3·8%	6·9%	0·8%	0·9%
(e) *Other (e.g. commissioning fees)*	5·8%	3·8%	6·6%	8·3%
Total earnings from Musical Composition	37·2%	35·7%	35·6%	40·7%
2. Other musical activities (e.g. teaching, performing, conducting, reviewing, etc.)	39·5%	37·1%	51·0%	37·3%
3. Non-Musical activities	23·3%	27·2%	13·4%	22·0%
	100·0%	100·0%	100·0%	100·0%

earning less than the average. Moreover, the percentage of earnings from different sources (Item II) must be treated with some caution because these are percentages based on average earnings. Nevertheless, they do give some general indication of the extent and manner of diversification among each type of composer. The significance of these percentages may become clearer in the course of reading this work, particularly the comparatively large proportion of earnings from musical composition now derived from performing and mechanical rights, alongside the very small percentage derived from sheet music. The table does not of course 'fill in all the boxes' in Virgil Thomson's classification, as no enquiry was made into unearned income.

Table 1.2, using data extracted from the same survey of composers' earnings, emphasizes the relatively small number of composers of all classes who can rely upon their earnings from musical composition as a significant proportion of their total earned income, more than half the composers sampled receiving as little as 20 per cent or less of their total earnings from this source.

Table 1.2   *Composers' earnings from musical composition as a percentage of their total earnings (1971)*

Percentage ranges	All composers	'Popular' composers	'Serious' composers	'Light' composers
1 less than 20%	53·0	55·0	61·0	43·0
2 20–80%	22·0	23·0	25·0	26·0
3 over 80%	25·0	22·0	14·0	31·0
	100·0%	100·0%	100·0%	100·0%

A second form of individual action is to try to *differentiate*[1] his type of music from that of others. This may be regarded as a transitional case between individual and collective action.[2] Certainly, there are striking examples of composers who have mainly relied on their own efforts in order to 'plug' their works, by exploiting their literary efforts or performing prowess. Before the development of copyright protection and greater division of labour in the production of new music, differentiation was also a partial protection against piracy. The composer's involvement in the production of his own work, as in the case of Rossini with his own operas, not only provided useful publicity, but allowed him supervision of the preparation and revision of the score and control over the issue of orchestral and vocal parts. Differentiation, however, is not a costless activity in terms of either time or money, particularly for the aspirant composer. The first

1. On the tactics of differentiation, see Paul Hindemith, *A Composer's World*, 1953. A typical remark in his spicy narrative: 'we do not want to be told that our scores are part of a heap of similar strugglers dumped on the far edge of our victim's writing desk and looked at with scornful ennui' (p.195).
2. See footnote 1, p.22.

requirement for differentiation is to obtain a hearing. Before a hearing can be obtained, the aspirant popular composer today must buy the services of a beat group, plus vocalist, a professional arranger of his music if needed, and can have a 45 r.p.m. 'Demo' Disc of two short songs recorded, all for not less than £50 (1973). In contrast, as we indicate in Chapter 5, a serious composer of larger chamber works and symphonic music has not only to find finance for scores and parts, but also for longer playing time provided by a much larger number of players. Sometimes, composers by dint of their personality and reputation can gather round them a devoted group of musicians who champion his works, the most notable case being the 'Britten circle', but it is open only to the exceptional few to be able to generate such interest in their activities that the public will pay not only for hearing first performances, but performances which reveal new works at what is really the 'research and development' stage of their creation.

2. *Co-operative Action*   It would be highly convenient to those in risky professions if they could find some means of insuring against losses and fluctuations in incomes, but no insurance company will enter into a contract to cover such risks when the probability of the amount and timing of loss cannot be estimated and the incidence of loss may be within the control of the individual, i.e. he could voluntarily incur losses and be compensated for them. What the composer can do, in common with other professions, is to look for others who are willing to share risks in return for a claim against the financial return. The obvious example of *risk-sharing* in the history of music is found in the financial relations between composer and publisher. Our historical survey will illustrate very clearly how the nature of risk-sharing operations between composer and publisher have changed both as a result of the influence of technology in the reproduction of music and of the alteration in the power structure in the market which accompanied technological change. Thus when publication consisted solely of sheet music used for public or private

performance, composers made individual bargains with publishers. The composer usually assigned copyright to the publisher who either paid him an outright sum or a royalty based on the copies of sheet music he was able to sell. Once the exploitation of mechanical and performing rights developed and the relative importance of sheet music as a source of income declined, the commercial relations which developed with radio and record companies required the standardization of contracts between publishers and composers for reasons fully explained in ensuing chapters.

As we have seen, the growing importance of the performing and mechanical rights in the course of this century brought with it the difficult problem of negotiation and enforcement of these rights which, for the individual composer, would mean prohibitive costs of collection and, with a broadcasting monopoly, the fear of unfavourable terms in the face of no alternative outlets. Though our historical survey shows that there were conflicts of interest between publishers and composers over the ways in which copyright in musical works should be exploited, both professions felt it necessary to join forces in order to take advantage of 'economies of scale' in royalty collection and to develop 'countervailing power' against powerful buyers such as the BBC and record companies. The most notable example of co-operation for these ends is found in the formation of the Performing Right Society in 1914, though, as we shall discover, the Society was formed largely on the initiative of music publishers.

This form of co-operation is now a world-wide phenomenon and gives rise to an important dilemma in economic policy. While it seems wholly reasonable to permit combinations of composers and publishers in order to protect their interests in a market in which monopoly or near-monopoly rights of radio and television are being conferred by the state on its own public corporations, the market conditions which emanate from this confrontation between powerful sellers and buyers may not be in the interests of 'final' consumers – the listening public – who want access to musical enjoyment on the cheapest terms possible.

It comes as no surprise to find that several governments with the final consumer in mind have instituted statutory machinery for reviewing the terms and conditions on which bargains between sellers and buyers of compositions are struck. In the case of Britain, this whole matter became the subject of considerable controversy after the Second World War, as we record in Chapter 4. It is beyond the scope of this book to speculate on future relations between governments and single national royalty collecting agencies which appear to operate rather like price-fixing cartels, but it has certainly come as a shock and a surprise to publishers and composers to find that the EEC authorities regard their societies' activities with some suspicion following the judgment that the German collecting agency (GEMA) was violating EEC cartel law.

3. *Collective Action* The commonest method by which producers of goods and services try to reduce risks is by combining among themselves so as to exercise control over price and output. Combinations among producers can range from complete mergers which reduce the number of firms to loose agreements of an informal kind confined to the exchange of information about impending price changes. A common characteristic of collective action among producers is the foundation of some form of trade association with the purpose, among other things, to promote good public relations and to act as a pressure group if members' interests are affected, for example, by government legislation.

Mergers on a scale sufficient to reduce 'music-producing firms' to a number where price and output would be affected by the actions of any one of them are not to be found among composers. Why? No attempt to give a full answer to this intriguing question can be offered in this contribution, but it is useful to speculate on the reasons for lack of merger arrangements as a prelude to a survey of the kinds of combination among composers which have actually obtained.

On the supply side, if the normal incentives operate, combination might promote economies in overhead expenditure, particularly capital investment, thus reducing costs per unit with longer production 'runs'. However, musical composition is a highly labour-intensive activity. The very idea of thinking in this way will suggest to indignant composers of all types of music that their motives in creating music are not dominated by profit maximizing and that if a composer desires to satisfy himself and receive the critical acclaim of his fellow-composers, he must retain independent control over his creations. As we have already indicated in discussing 'product differentiation', there may also be sound commercial sense in this view, for the close identity of the composer with his creation may be the 'hall mark' which guarantees him an audience, though in the case of 'pop' music the artist or the artist/composer may be a more important 'draw'. Finally, it may be that we are concentrating too much attention on the 'creative' rather than the 'exploitive' stage of operations and should be looking for mergers among publishers and others concerned with the 'buying in' of the services of composers and the marketing of their creations. However, as we show in Chapter 5, the position of the publisher is a complicated one, and, even if mergers and take-overs have taken place, publishing remains a highly competitive business for all kinds of composition.

The need to co-operate with one another and with publishers to protect their copyright and its exploitation reduced the costs of professional and commercial contact between composers and might very well have led to a situation in which the Performing Right Society took over the function of a 'trade association' for composers. Though composers have not sought to operate a 'production cartel' which would control output of music as a means of safeguarding their economic position, 'pop' composers in particular have been vociferous in their criticism of the music policies of bodies such as the BBC which they claim have unduly favoured foreign, particularly American, music. The PRS, however, represents publishers as well as composers, and the publishers' interest lies in the marketing of potentially successful

music irrespective of national origin. Secondly, the PRS represents foreign collecting agencies who are exploiting rights of
overseas composers. While these reasons are sufficient to explain why composers have had to rely on the setting up of
separate organizations, such as the Composers' Guild and Songwriters' Guild, to promote British music, the PRS, having already undergone extensive investigation in the 1950s during the
'Battle of the Copyright Bill' (which led to the Copyright Act
1956), was not likely to assume a role which might attract the
accusation that it supported restrictive practices, such as 'quota'
measures against overseas composers.

An outstanding feature in twentieth-century economic and
social policy is the widespread use of government subsidies as a
means of modifying the effects of market forces. The general
case for subsidies rests on the view that the benefits to society
are not fully reflected in the scale of operation in, say, a particular industry as would result from ordinary commercial operation. To prove the case, it must be shown that realizing these
benefits by offering a subsidy will leave society 'better off',
after allowing for the costs incurred by society as a result of providing government support. Without investigating the refine-
ments of cost-benefit analysis, it will no doubt be clear to the
reader that evaluation of these costs and benefits not only pre-
sents difficult technical problems, but is beset by the special
pleading of interested parties. The prospect of direct state support, on top of legislative measures which may favour the commercial interests of a particular industry (e.g. tariff policy), adds
further impetus to collective action within the industry and the co-
ordination through a trade association or equivalent body in order
to have the persuasive case ready at the appropriate moment.

The question of state patronage of the Arts and of composition
in particular is regarded as beyond the scope of this work,[1] if

1. One of us has written already on this matter. See A. T. Peacock, 'Public
Patronage and Music: An Economist's View', *Three Banks Review*, March 1968;
'Welfare Economics and Public Subsidies to the Arts', *Manchester School of
Economic Studies*, December 1969; 'Justifying the Subsidy', *Opera*, May 1971.

only because patronage has only exercised a minor influence on the market for musical composition as a whole, though the BBC has clearly played a major role throughout its existence in supporting new 'serious' music. Certainly with growing support for the creative arts emanating from the Arts Council of Great Britain, serious composers, at least, through the Composers' Guild, have an understandable interest in how that support is allocated. Thus our review of methods of collective action by composers would be incomplete, if it were not noted that the incentives for collective action among such composers are likely to be strengthened by the growing dependence of live performance by orchestras, opera and ballet companies on public funds.

*

Two abiding impressions are left from conversation with composers and from a perusal of their writings on the market for their music. The first is that, compared with their eighteenth- and early nineteenth-century counterparts, they are typically totally unprepared at the beginning of their careers for the problems they will encounter in making a living. Aaron Copland[1] must express the experience of many of his fellow-composers when he wrote: 'Looking backward to that time (1924), I am rather amazed at my own ignorance of musical conditions in America. I mean, of course, conditions as they affected composers. How a composer managed to get his compositions performed or published and how he expected to make a living were equally mysterious.' Those composers who undergo a testing professional training – and by no means all of them finish up writing so-called 'serious' music – might be better served by their universities or academies if they were given at least some indication of the economic and social environment in which they will find themselves, and some realistic advice on how to market

1. Aaron Copland, *The New Music 1900–60*, London, 1968, p.156. Puccini's first librettist, Ferdinando Fonata wrote of him: 'To leave the Conservatorio with the moral and material patent of maestro meant not to end but to begin a terrible struggle in that vast conservatorio which is the world.' Quoted in *Letters of Giacomo Puccini* (Ed. Guiseppe Adami), London, 1931, p.27.

as well as to score their works. The second is the suspicion at the workings of the market which permeates composers' writing on their social and economic position,[1] the origin of this suspicion being perhaps not unconnected with the traumatic shock of total unpreparedness which we have just considered. This is understandable, for there must be few professions who have to face up to the fact that their professional evaluations of their creations are so much at variance with the judgment of the consumer expressed in what the latter is willing to pay. Furthermore, if a composer seeks to maximize the relative proportion of his income derived from composition, he is likely to have to engage at least part-time in manufacturing 'musical wallpaper', however much he may prefer to be satisfying rather than compromising his artistic standards. Even the experiences of composers of all kinds in totalitarian countries have not reconciled them to the view that a market system may serve them better than a 'command economy'. At least in the market economy the composer can investigate *alternative* sources of financial support, whereas in the 'command economy' one arch-monopolist dictates *both* what kind of music a composer must compose and what rewards he is to receive. To blame the market system for the disparity between the cultural standards of the composer and those of the consumer and the resultant paucity of rewards for the former, is like blaming a gun for murder. It has been well said that 'if anything is wrong with the arts, we should seek the cause in ourselves, not in our economy'.[2]

Whatever composers' attitudes may be to their market environment, the striking fact remains that in twentieth-century Britain they have managed by a variety of means already described, to develop countervailing power in order to protect themselves against potentially influential purchasers and against the threat to their livelihood resulting from technical innovations.

1. For evidence, see Peacock, *op. cit.*, *Three Banks Review*, March 1968.
2. Tibor Scitovsky, 'What's Wrong with the Arts is What's Wrong with Society', *Papers and Proceedings of the American Economic Association*, May 1972, p.69.

They have done so by well known forms of individual and collective action and by co-operation with publishers and others with whom they have made common cause. In short, composers have displayed an intelligent appreciation of their own economic interests. No one need think any the less of them for that.

2
The Music Market
1900-14

Introduction

In April 1905 the nineteen members of the Music Publishers' Association announced that they would not accept any more music for publication nor enter into any new contracts for payments to artistes and singers of new publications. Given that the main source of income for music publishers, and the composers who depended on them, were the profits from concert promotions and the sale of sheet music, this self-denying abstinence from their normal business activities indicated that under prevailing conditions continuation of these activities was impossible. The publishers had been driven into this action as '. . . a consequence of the present deplorable position of music composers, and of the music publishing and retail trade, brought about by the want of protection against music pirates . . .'[1]

The reaction of music publishers and composers to their exposed position was to form a 'Musical Defence League', whose main object '. . . was to drive the fact into the heads of the general public, and simultaneously into the heads of several very dense Members of Parliament, that composers were not able to live upon suction but required as much nourishment to keep body and soul together as any other members of the community . . .'[2]

The piracy that was causing so much concern in music circles was the practice of selling pirated copies of songs and other music through street hawkers and the difficulty of discovering

1. William Boosey, *Fifty Years of Music*, London, 1931, p.115.
2. *Ibid.*, p.113.

any substantial person against whom to take infringement action. The pirated copies could be produced at very little cost because the original edition could be photographed or reproduced by the litho process in any back room and put on sale for as little as 2d per copy within a week of the issue of the authorized printing. The pirating of musical works was, therefore, much easier and more profitable than the illegal copying of books. The music publishers waged a constant battle against the pirates, whose activities were not only ruinous to their business but also directly prejudiced authors as well, through the loss of their royalties on the sale of copies and less directly through depreciation of the value of their copyrights.

The Copyright Act 1842, then still in force, had the defect that it did not provide summary penalties against misappropriation of copyright. The only way to proceed against theft of copyright was by way of an application to the Civil Court for an injunction and damages. While these were always granted, the recovery of costs and damages by this lengthy procedure was often impossible in practice, the infringers being 'men of straw'.

The campaign against these practices ended triumphantly with the enactment of the Music (Summary Proceedings) Act 1902 and the Music Copyright Act 1906, which provided summary methods of procedure against the production of infringing copies and their distributions.[1]

The publication of sheet music, under these conditions, continued for some twenty-five years more to be the main support of musical creation. Already, however, the commercial gramophone recording, its destined but then unheralded successor, was beginning to come into use, while it would have been difficult at the turn of the century to foresee how another, and at that time in Britain, largely unexploited form of copyright, that of public performance, was to become for many composers and publishers the predominant outlet for their activity.[2]

1. The name of T. P. O'Connor MP, an ardent defender of authors' rights, deserves to be remembered in this connection.
2. The gramophone or panatrope had the defect, for the purposes of public performance, of being at that period hand-wound.

The first British Act in protection of copyright, that of 1709, had not covered performance, and the first Act which did this was the Dramatic Copyright Act 1833, commonly known as Bulwer Lytton's Act, which was of limited purport in that its provisions extended only to dramatic pieces at places of entertainment. The Copyright Act 1842 enlarged the provisions of the Act of 1833 to cover musical compositions, and although it too applied only to performances at places of entertainment the Courts interpreted this condition very liberally and in effect extended it to performance in public generally.

For reasons which will be discussed later, the public performance right in musical works before 1914 was not in fact exploited outside the field of dramatic or stage works. The popular concert, promoted for the most part by publishers themselves, derived its profitability from box office charges and the stimulation of sales of sheet copies. Exploitation of the right to perform in public was regarded as inimical to the main interest of the music creators, that is sale of copies. Moreover, even in advance of such exploitation, it had been given a bad name by unscrupulous persons who purchased the legal right for the sole purpose of enforcing penalties against its unauthorized use by unwitting performers; penalties which had been fixed by the Act of 1833 at 40s per performance. The practice led to the passing of the Copyright (Musical Compositions) Acts of 1882 and 1888, which required the proprietor of the copyright in a published musical work who wished to exercise the right of public performance to print on the title page of every published copy of the work a notice specifically reserving the right. The question of costs or penalties, if it arose, was left to the Court's discretion.

However, before the enactment of the Copyright Act 1911, the specific reservation of the public performance right in nondramatic music was not usually made. In fact, until 1912, when the Copyright Act of 1911 came into force, it was not the practice of most British publishers of popular music to reserve that right but rather to print on copies a notice such as 'This song may be sung in public without fee or licence.'

The Copyright Act of 1911, which followed Britain's adherence to the Berlin Convention on Copyright of 1908, codified and repealed nearly all the provisions of the preceding Acts in protection of copyright, and in particular the Acts of 1882 and 1888 requiring notice of reservation of the public performance right. The principal rights granted under the 1911 Act to the creators of original literary, dramatic, musical and artistic work (and transferable by assignment to another party, or subject to licence) were:

1 the right to reproduce the work in any material form, including the form of a mechanical recording;
2 the right of publication;
3 the right of performance in public;
4 the right to authorize other persons to do these acts.

In retrospect, the music pirates proved but a short-lived threat to the livelihood of composers and publishers, and music piracy may seem an unusual subject with which to begin a study of the major influences governing the economics of musical composition between 1900 and 1970. In serving to highlight the ease with which the right in an intangible property can be stolen or misappropriated, the dependence of the composer on effective copyright protection for the carrying-on of his profession, and the frequent necessity for him to resort to joint action with others in his group, the affair of the music pirates contains many of the distinctive features present in the composer's approach to his market. The only major element absent from this story is that of technical change, by which is meant changes in the media through which musical composition is communicated, the methods of its execution and the location and size of the market. In all these areas, changes were occurring in the years immediately prior to the First World War which were to be of great significance to composers and music publishers.

This history is concerned with the exploitation of the four rights enumerated above, and the changing economic and technical conditions under which they have been exercised. The period covered ranges from the passing of the 1911 Copyright Act to 1970. During this time the 1911 legislation, though revised in 1956, has been the composer's protective 'umbrella'.

The Nature of the Market

The most important point to emphasize about the music market before 1914 is that it was not stable. Much of the discussion on the economic position of the composer in the inter-war period (1918 – 39) has tended to assume that the composer had always had a guaranteed, reliable outlet for the sale of his music before the First World War. In fact, the nineteenth century had witnessed many changes in the composer's market and in the contractual relationships through which he approached the market. As a recreational activity, the demand for music increased markedly with the growth in leisure time available to the British middle class from around the 1850s, and to the working class from the 1870s. This increased demand was expressed in the great popularity of public concerts, private recitals, the music hall, musical comedy, the seaside concert party, incidental theatre music and competitive music festivals. Reflecting what Mackerness has described as '. . . the variety and profusion of English musical life . . .'[1] was the increase in the numbers of professional composers, music teachers, conductors, directors and players together with a vast body of practising, but amateur musicians, both in '. . . the peaceful domestic atmosphere of the mid-Victorian home . . .' and in the local orchestral and choral societies and brass bands. It may be, although there are no figures to prove this conclusively, that in the mid- and late-Victorian periods a greater proportion of the population than either before or since was actively involved in music-making both as amateurs and professionals. Music, prior to the First World War, played a large and vital role in English social life.

If the market for music was growing up till 1914, it was not however a unified market. Composers, as today, were split

1. E. D. Mackerness, *A Social History of English Music*, London, 1964, p.206.

between serious and popular music. The interests of the music publishing firms reflected this. Novello, for example, specialized in sacred music, instructional books, and standard textbooks; Chappell's catalogue contained a high proportion of dance music, whilst Boosey traded mainly in songs, ballads and duets.[1] Nor was the market dependent simply on growing leisure time. In publishing, a combination of factors helped to widen the market for printed music. The degree of protection given by the 1842 Copyright Act reduced the risk involved in publishing, whilst the abolition of the paper duties lowered the cost of sheet music. The move by publishers like Novello into printing to overcome the restrictive practices of the London printers worked in the same direction.[2] Besides increased leisure, industrialization brought other benefits to the musical public in cheaper and better musical instruments. Mechanical improvements and large scale production techniques placed the pianoforte within both the musical skills and incomes of a wide public. The inculcation of these skills gave employment to a large body of music teachers, and home performances – with accompanist – created a demand for the drawing room ballad which was met by composers and publishers with the 'royalty song'. In the absence of the phonograph and the wireless, the Victorian musical evening stands as the epitome of Victorian music-making activity.

As far as public performance was concerned, the absence of the mass media kept the market fragmented and scattered. No matter how large the total demand for music, the actual audience available to a composer at any one moment in time was relatively small. Music, dance and concert halls were all restricted in their capacity. Even the three largest London concert halls, the Albert Hall, the Queen's Hall and St James's Hall seated only 8,000, 3,000 and 2,000 respectively. Moreover, by the end of the century there were signs that public concert attendance was declining. Novello lost money on their Albert Hall concerts

1. 1928 Copyright Royalty (Mechanical Musical Instruments) Inquiry, see R. Moritz.
2. E. D. Mackerness, *op. cit.*, p.176.

and even the once packed 'Monday Pops' and 'Saturday Pops' which Chappell had promoted in St James's Hall were losing custom by the 1890s. The series ended in 1898. William Boosey, the publisher and concert promoter, blamed competition from free charity concerts for the decline, but, though this may have been a factor contributing to the promoter's financial difficulties, it seems much more likely that other causes were at work. One reason, which has been suggested for the diminished popularity of the public concert, is that the location of the main concert halls in city centres left them increasingly isolated from a suburban middle class and daily commuting weakened the incentive to return to town to attend evening concerts. It is doubtful if the growth of suburban living was the predominant reason, at least before the First World War. The miseries of long distance commuting were really only apparent after the 1920s with the development of 'Metroland' and its Southern Railway equivalents. On the contrary, improvements in urban transport in the 1870s – omnibuses, trains and then the Brompton Railway – might have been expected to bring back the clerks of Clapham or Holloway to the West End. The more obvious division of function between the City as a place of work and the West End as a place of entertainment made the return journey a different one – and relatively easy for the denizens of North and West London after the opening of the Piccadilly and Central London Railways. Moreover, although the concert hall declined, suburbanization did not prevent the luxury restaurants, supper rooms, hotels, music halls and theatres from flourishing. Alternative explanations favour a rather more complex picture of the leisure market and the public's demand for music. Public demand – or at least a critical middle and upper class section of it – was shifting towards entertainments offering greater variety (as well as food and drink) in more luxurious surroundings. The concert halls of an earlier generation were unwilling or unable to adapt their fabric to the public's evident desire for clean electric lighting and electric fans. Gas lighting and naphtha stage-lighting created an unendurable fug which was unacceptable to delicate ladies, and growing social acceptability of smoking in public made matters worse. Ladies would not go to 'smoking concerts'; gentlemen would not go to places where cigars were frowned upon. If the atmosphere and amenities of public concerts were relatively poor, the musical performances were often worse. The entertainment boom of the 1870s threw up a host of mediocre conductors and soloists who often assumed bogus foreign names or qualifications. Indifferent musicians found it relatively easy to transfer their 'talents' from one sector of the entertainment world to another, and, as George Bernard Shaw remarked, bad music inevitably drove out good. The movement, amongst serious musicians, to establish professional examining bodies and the concern about the lack of conservatoires in London in comparison with other musical capitals, betray contemporary anxiety about the standard of public performance.

The public concert drew its support from what was, socially, a relatively narrow audience. Mainly patronized by sections of the middle and upper classes it was extremely vulnerable to any change in their preferences. And these were the groups which possessed sufficient income to effectively express their preferences. Musical instruments, tuition, and by the early 1900s the gramophone, were all within their grasp and their more comfortable domestic surroundings made private music making an acceptable alternative.

By contrast to the declining public concert, the music hall, a socially unifying form of entertainment in the late nineteenth century, attracted a large slice of the custom arising from the post-1870 boom and was the main medium for the transmission of popular music. The overall picture of Victorian musical activity is a paradoxical one, with serious music, at least in its public aspect through the outlet of the concert hall, apparently in decline, whilst popular music enjoyed buoyant demand.

The Composer and his Income: The Publishing Right

Amidst these signs of growth and decay what was the composer's position with respect to his market, and what were his sources of income? In exploiting the market the composer, before 1914, did so as an individual. Despite the grouping of performing musicians into trade unions in the early 1890s[1] and the development of professional bodies in teaching and examining, composers, as a group, did not combine. Their entry to the market was as individuals and their main contractual relationship was with the music publisher. Apart from income derived from '. . . the whirlpool of teaching and examining which devours so many of our talents . . .'[2] and from conducting and directing, the main source of earnings almost certainly lay in sales of sheet music and royalties on them. Payment to composers by publishers through percentage royalties on the sale of sheet music was a means of payment developed during the nineteenth century. It was pioneered by John Boosey in an attempt to spread the risks of publishing between the publisher and the composer. Prior to the introduction of the royalty payment the composer had received a lump sum for the assignment of his copyright to the publisher. As William Boosey put it,

Many instances occurred of the purchase of valuable copyrights, particularly operas, at the price of a mere song, which works often resulted in a very big profit to the publisher. On the other hand, the publisher would pay a heavy price for subsequent works the purchase of which would result in a dead loss. The results were obviously unsatisfactory both to composer and publisher.[3]

The royalty system of payment as it developed applied to all forms of music. However, the exploitation of the publishing right by means of the royalty payment was much more widespread in Britain than in most other European countries, where performance right royalties were the main source of income. In France for example, a collecting society, the Société des Auteurs,

1. Two musicians' unions were formed in the 1890s, the Amalgamated Musicians Union in 1893, and the National Orchestral Union of Professional Musicians in 1891. In 1921 they joined together as the Musicians Union.
2. P. A. Scholes, *The Mirror of Music*, London, 1947, Vol.1, p.473.
3. William Boosey, *op. cit.*, p.23.

Compositeurs et Editeurs de Musique (SACEM), had been founded as early as 1851. This contrasts with the situation in Britain where, for reasons which will be discussed below, a collecting society for performance royalties, the Performing Right Society, was not established until 1914.

Although it is not possible to chart the growth and subsequent decline in sheet music sales precisely, or to examine the size of composers' earnings from this source, some features of the sheet music market can be established. Cheap published editions of music date from the 1840s, and the market for sheet music appears to have grown up to the turn of the century. Its decline thereafter was due initially to the slump caused by the 'gutter piracy' of 1903 – 4[1] and, more serious in the long run, competition from the gramophone. The talents which the popular royalty song demanded from composers and lyric writers have been described as 'an instinct for commonplace sentiments'.[2] Some idea of the results of the successful tapping of these sentiments may be gained from the sheet music sales for particular songs. The patriotic fervour of the Boer War, for example, raised sales of 'Soldiers of the Queen' to 238,000 copies in 1898. This was a figure which Frederick Day, the Managing Director of the publishing firm of Francis, Day & Hunter Ltd, thought '. . . was typical of successful copies prior to the mechanical industry'[3] and considered sales of 200,000 copies equal to a 'hit'. Another hit based on popular sentiment, 'That Old Fashioned Mother of Mine', brought out in the 1920s, had combined sheet music and record sales of 704,000 copies, from which Lawrence Wright, the composer and publisher, received a total income of £4,914. Large as this may seem, only £377 came from mechanical rights, a feature of the music market in the 1920s which caused great indignation to be felt by composers and publishers.

Hits alone did not guarantee the composer an income from sheet music sales prior to 1914, even at the popular end of the

---

1. 1928 Copyright Royalty (Mechanical Musical Instruments) Inquiry, evidence of Frederick Day.   2. E. D. Mackerness, *op. cit.*, p.232.
3. 1928 Copyright Royalty (etc.) Inquiry.

market. Much depended on the royalty sharing agreement with the publisher. A new composer with no successes to his credit was in a particularly poor bargaining position, and even a well established writer could still be expected to bear some of the costs and risks involved in publishing in a low royalty percentage. What were these costs and risks? In the first place there was the ever present risk that a song might flop. William Boosey reckoned that only one song in forty which his firm published could really be described as a success,[1] and the cost of publishing and pushing the less successful songs had to be borne by the more successful. The costs involved in popularizing a song included engaging singers, concert promotion, newspaper advertising and maintaining travellers throughout the country.[2] These costs could reach substantial amounts. Lawrence Wright, for example, claimed to be spending £1,000 per week during the summer of 1928 'plugging' his firm's publications through dance and concert bands in the main seaside resorts. On 'Among my Souvenirs', a song which brought his firm only £1,085 he spent £4,000 on publicity, which included sending lantern slides and words of the song '. . . to every picture house in the country' as well as a free issue of band parts. Excluding simple failures, the composer of popular music was also required to bear a share of promotional costs and, apart from the past commercial record of his work, the level of royalty was determined by three other factors. The first was advertising costs: as Frederick Day said, '. . . the less money spent on advertising, the more the composer gets in royalty'.[3] The second involved a judgment by the publisher on the quality of the song, with popular sheet music receiving a lower percentage royalty than the concert ballad 'which has more intrinsic merit'.[4] The third factor, partially related to the second, operated in the market for classical music where slower selling classical works were subsidized from 'ephemeral novelty'[5] profits. Exactly what these

1. *Ibid.*, evidence of William Boosey.   2. *Ibid.*
3. *Ibid.*, evidence of Frederick Day.   4. *Ibid.*
5. E. D. Mackerness, *op. cit.*, p.177.

trade arrangements meant for individual composers it is impossible to say, but what is interesting is that many of these features of the composer's publishing right were to be carried over after the decline in the importance of that right as a source of income, to his mechanical recording and performing rights.

How important was the publisher to the composer before 1914? The service provided by the publisher was essentially a distributive one, and he traded his expert knowledge of the music market for the composer's copyright. There was in fact no compulsion on the composer to take his work to a publisher. Composers could have kept their work in manuscript and hired it out, or they could have gone to individual printers and had it printed. The administrative costs involved in hiring out manuscripts, together with the absence of publicity, made this a dubious recipe for success. Many classical composers never published and died leaving a mountain of manuscript from which they had secured no return. Likewise, independent printing left the composer to carry all the costs of failure and distribution and publicity as well. In practice then, the only realistic approach was for the composer to put his work in the hands of a publisher. Certainly until 1914, and probably into the 1920s, it was possible for publishers to maintain that '. . . publication is vital, otherwise there is no market at all'.[1]

Performing and Mechanical Recording Rights

'. . . I was gradually becoming aware that, probably, eventually a composer's performing rights might be even more valuable than his publishing rights . . .'.[2] This recognition by William Boosey, the publisher, of the growing importance of the third of the basic rights granted to composers in the 1911 Copyright Act

1. 1928 Copyright Royalty etc. Inquiry, evidence of the Musical Copyright Defence Association. An alternative method, most commonly found in popular music, was for the composer to sell his copyright, or at least the music hall singing rights, to the variety stars who featured the songs on their programmes. And, as today, some artists composed their own songs.
2. William Boosey, *op. cit.*, p.175.

reflected the changed circumstances of the music market evident before 1914. How did this change come about? The predominance of the publishing right as a source of composers' income and as a means for publishers to exploit the music market had been shown to be exceptionally vulnerable to piracy. More serious in its long-run implications for reliance on exploitation of the publishing right was the growth of what contemporaries called 'mechanical music'.

Edison's phonograph appeared in 1877 but, although music was frequently used in his experiments and public demonstrations, the poor quality of reproduction and the limited quantity of music produced, meant that the phonograph remained till the early 1890s '. . . a surprisingly clever and amusing toy',[1] and the 'phonophile' a somewhat eccentric enthusiast. A series of innovations including Berliner's wax discs (1895), the clock spring motor (1897), shellac discs (1904), and double sided discs (1905) soon converted the novelty phonograph into the commercially successful gramophone. Continuing difficulties with sound reproduction and the high cost of records – Patti records of 'Home Sweet Home' cost £1 each in 1906 – limited the initial impact of the innovation on sheet music sales. With mass production techniques and aggressive selling, the price of gramophones and records soon came into direct competition with sales of sheet music and the problem for composers and publishers alike was how to adjust to his new situation. Two solutions seemed to offer themselves: one was to ensure that the gramophone industry paid for the raw material – musical composition – on which it so heavily relied, and the other was to seek out a new source of income in the composer's public performing right.

The Performing Right

Before the 1911 Copyright Act and the development of the gramophone the attitude of music publishers to the collection of

---

1. P. Scholes, *op. cit.*, Plate 111 quoting advertisement in the *Illustrated London News*.

fees for performing rights had, in most cases, been one of out-
right hostility. As William Boosey himself frankly admitted,
'. . . I considered that the payment of a fee for the performance
of new music, and even established music, was calculated to
injure seriously the sales of established favourites, and was very
detrimental to the popularizing of new works . . .'.[1] With the
appearance of mechanical music Boosey had begun to change his
opinion of the value of performing right fees by the early 1900s.
As already mentioned,[2] the French music publishers relied quite
heavily on fees from public performances, and with Britain's
accession to the Berne Convention in 1886,[3] French (and other
foreign) composers had their national rights protected in British
territory. The French composers' national society – SACEM –
took advantage of this convention and employed an agent in the
UK for the protection of the performing rights in French music
and for the collection of royalties for public performances.[4]
British publishers and composers did not follow this lead, which
resulted in 'the anomalous situation . . . where the French composer is securing payment for the use of his works, whilst the
British composer in his own country went unrewarded'.[5] Why
this curious anomaly should have arisen is not at all clear. C. F.
James in his study of the Performing Right Society thought 'that
some explanation . . . may be found in the unsatisfactory state of
our Copyright Law prior to 1911 . . .'.[6] This however does not
seem a satisfactory explanation, for although the law before
1911 stated that a performance 'to be an infringement of copyright has to be represented at a place of dramatic entertainment'[7]
this condition had been interpreted by the Courts as being ful-
filled if the performance was at any place in public 'since to hold
otherwise would deprive an author of his rights to the profits of
his work'.[8] A more likely reason for the failure to collect per-

1. William Boosey, *op. cit.*, p.174.   2. See pp.8–9.
3. With the passing of the International Copyright Act, 1886.
4. C. F. James, *The Story of the PRS*, London, 1951, p.16.
5. *Ibid*.   6. *Ibid*.
7. Copinger and Skone James, *Copyright*, London, 1965, paragraph 513.
8. *Ibid*.

forming right royalties lies in the contractual relationship which existed between the composer and his publisher. Normally the composer assigned all performing rights to the publisher, but publishers used these rights in a purely defensive manner for the purpose of controlling or even preventing performances from borrowed, second-hand or hire-copies of sheet music. The only exception to this arrangement was where a composer commissioned a publisher and retained the performing right for himself. One other factor which prevented the composer from asserting his performing right was his individually weak bargaining position with the publisher, and the related absence of a united organization of British composers akin to the French national society. Although publishers emphasized the defensive aspect of the performing right, their control of the right was ultimately connected with their desire to profit from concert promotion. For the composer, concert performances of his work were merely a form of advertisement which would enhance his sales of sheet music and therefore his income from royalties. For the publisher, however, sales of concert seats directly increased his income as a promoter, so that he retained all the direct benefits of the performing right, as well as gaining from his share of profits on any enhanced sales of sheet music. So long as the music publishers controlled the majority of concert outlets, and so long as sheet music sales remained buoyant, both classical and popular music were open to commercial exploitation. With the decline in concert attendances, signalled by the growing losses which those publishing firms who owned or leased concert halls were suffering in the 1890s, and the threat to sheet music sales from gramophone records, evident by the early 1900s, reliance on these marketing arrangements was no longer possible. These developments, as much as the enhanced legislative safeguards given to the exercise of the performing right in 1911, help to explain the development of a growing interest amongst composers and publishers in making arrangements for the protection of their performing rights.

Led by the publishers, the campaign for the exploitation of

the performing right resulted in March 1914 in the formation of
the Performing Right Society. Its object were to protect copyright music against infringement by unauthorized public performance and to grant permission for public performance on payment of a licence royalty. The right which the music publishers
and writers vested in the PRS was that of non-dramatic performance in public, and, since the Copyright Act does not distinguish between dramatic and non-dramatic performance, the
latter is defined in the Society's Articles of Association. While,
accordingly, the PRS does not collect royalties on stage performances as such, it does collect royalties on the performance in
theatres of incidental or interval music. Also, since cinemato-
graphic films are not regarded as dramatic works, the Society
collects from cinemas both in regard to the musical accompaniment to films and to other music. Although it had almost in-
variably been the practice of composers and lyric authors, when
making terms with a publisher, to assign to the publisher the
whole of their copyright, including the right of public performance, the publishers agreed that composers and authors who
joined the Society should share in the revenue of the Society.
The distribution of performance royalties between the various
interested parties (composer, author, arranger – if any – publisher, sub-publisher – if any) evolved into a complex system,
but the basic rule which has survived all these vicissitudes is that
the combined share of all the creative parties shall never be less
than 50 per cent of the total royalties and the share of the original publisher and his foreign sub-publishers, if any, more than
50 per cent of the total royalties. Once the publishers agreed to
vest the performing rights of a large repertoire of copyright
music in the Society, the foundation was laid for the commercial
exploitation of these rights. In 1914 only the foundation was
laid, and the subsequent problems involved in the continued
existence of a viable Society will be further examined in
Chapter 3.

The Mechanical Recording Right

If in 1914 the struggle to assert the composer's performing right
was just getting under way, the campaign over mechanical
rights could be said to have been partly resolved, though by no
means to the satisfaction of composers and publishers. The
legacy of history on mechanical rights was an unfortunate one.
In 1886, when the original Berne Convention for the protection
of literary and artistic works was signed, the only means for
reproducing music mechanically were musical boxes and Bar-
bary Organs. Manufacture of these instruments was a Swiss
industry, and the provision of the Berne Convention that mechanical reproduction of music should be no infringement of copyright was of some value to the Swiss industry whilst it did little
harm to music composers in general. With the development of a
range of mechanical devices such as perforated rolls, cylinders
and discs, and the subsequent improvement in reproduction
standards, composers and publishers formed a different view of
the effects of 'mechanical music'. Actions were brought in
British courts to test whether these instruments were or were
not an infringement of the composers' copyrights in the works
reproduced. In 1899 the Appeal Court in England ruled that
reproduction of musical works by these instruments did not in-
fringe the composer's copyright. Thus protected by the law, a
sizeable industry developed in Britain for the manufacture of
mechanical instruments. Their commercial interest clearly favoured a continuance of the existing legal position. The revision
of the Berne Convention at Berlin in 1908 resulted in the inclusion of a requirement that signatories of the revised convention
should give protection to composers against reproduction of
their works by mechanical means. In 1909 a Committee of the
Board of Trade was established to consider how British copyright law might best be altered so as to conform with international requirements. Composers and publishers argued before
the committee in favour of the unrestricted protection stipulated

by the revised convention. Their arguments met with little favour from the manufacturing interests which, whilst recognizing the composers' right to remuneration, objected to composers being given unlimited powers either to permit or prohibit the reproduction of their works. The approach recommended by the manufacturers was ominously similar to the contemporary solution to mechanical rights in the United States. Traditionally weaker in its protection of copyright property, the law in the United States allowed manufacturing interests compulsory powers to acquire licences to reproduce works by mechanical means on payment of a fixed royalty. Behind this principle lay the fear that, in the absence of a compulsory licence, the largest and wealthiest firms in the record industry would, by making exclusive licensing agreements with composers, obtain a monopoly in the most popular works. It was not a view shared by the Board of Trade committee for, with the exception of Trevor Williams, the Managing Director of the Gramophone Company, the committee reported in favour of giving composers full control of the reproduction of their works by mechanical instruments. Thus far events had run favourably for composers, but when the Copyright Bill made its way through '. . . those lethal chambers which are called House of Commons Committees . . .'[1] the gramophone industry's plea that unrestricted composers' rights would be seriously damaging in an 'infant industry' resulted in the compromise solution embodied in Section 19 of the 1911 Copyright Act. The effect of this section was to compel a composer, if he had granted a licence to one person to reproduce his works mechanically, to grant to any other person a licence to reproduce the same work upon payment of a statutory royalty. Although the composer was not compelled to grant a licence to more than one person, any other manufacturer could reproduce the work mechanically on complying with certain formalities and paying the royalty fixed by the Act. Without the right to make exclusive licensing agreements the composer

1. William Boosey, *op. cit.*, p.146.

could not act as a free agent. Worrying as this restriction was, even more alarming in view of changes which were to take place in the record industry after 1911 were the level of royalty and the conditions surrounding it. That level was set from 1914 at 5 per cent 'on the ordinary retail selling price of the contrivance . . .' with a provision that the royalty should in no case be less than $\frac{1}{2}$d for each musical work. In the case of double-sided records (which first appeared in 1905) where two composers contributed one musical work apiece, the royalty was divided at $2\frac{1}{2}$ per cent each. Nor was the composer the sole recipient of the royalty, for it had to be shared with the lyric writer and publisher.

What was the effect of these provisions when translated into the economic circumstances of the record market? Already by 1911 the retail selling price of records had dropped considerably from the novelty pioneer days and a ten-inch record with one composition now sold at 3s 6d and a twelve-inch record at 5s 6d, giving a royalty payment of 2·1d and 3·3d respectively. Although sheet music royalties at average rates of $12\frac{1}{2}$ per cent were more than double the record royalty, the selling price was lower at 2s per copy or a royalty of 2·9d, so that the overall position as far as the composer was concerned was not dissimilar. After 1918 however this situation of rough parity changed drastically. In order to compete with the growing popularity of records, music publishers were forced to cut the price of sheet music and, by the mid 1920s, sixpenny editions were widespread. This growth in the popularity of records stemmed in part from improvements in sound recording and reproduction, especially the replacement in 1926 of mechanical recording by an all-electric system of sound recording and reproduction. With electrical reproduction involving an electrical sound box, valve amplifier and loud speaker, all the old problems of adjusting sound-boxes, tone arms and amplifying horns disappeared. Record manufacturers were now able to increase the playing time of records and thereby squeeze more compositions on to each side. On top of this wave of innovations a fierce competitive struggle broke out between gramophone manufacturers, and by 1927 the ten-inch and twelve-inch records were not merely lower priced, at 3s and 4s 6d respectively, than in 1911 but now carried two compositions instead of one. The composers' royalties suffered accordingly, and in 1927 the Musical Copyright Defence Association, an organization comprising composers, authors, copyright owners and publishers took advantage of the provision in section 19(3) of the Copyright Act of 1911 to have the Board of Trade institute a public inquiry into the rate of royalty on records. The result of this inquiry will be further considered in Chapter 3.

3

The Music Market 1914-39

The machines have seized us, devoured us, and cast us forth again in a thousand duplications . . .[1]

I am getting tired of the constant girding at 'our mechanized age'. It is a very pleasant age, and the machines are going to make it a great deal pleasanter . . . It is no more good to try to stop the progress of the machines in art than it was any good for the weavers of Bolton to break the machines in the eighteenth century.[2]

Introduction

The conflicting attitudes to the mechanization of music expressed in these two quotations symbolize the turmoil in the music market in the inter-war period. The diffusion of three developments: the cinema, the wireless and the gramophone radically altered the position of the composer and other members of the music industry with respect to the market. In addition to these innovations, the First World War also added a further upset to the position of music in British life.

The First World War

On the eve of the First World War it had become clear that reliance on the sale of sheet music for the commercial exploitation of the music market was no longer tenable. The search for

1. George Dyson, 'The Future of Music', *Musical Times*, February 1935.
2. Letter in the *Musical Times*, July 1929.

alternative sources of income in performing and mechanical rights was not free from difficulty. The first meeting of the new Performing Right Society was held on 1 April 1914, and the infant organization could hardly be said to have been well established by the time war broke out in August. As far as the composer's mechanical rights were concerned, although the principle of royalty payment had been settled by the Copyright Act of 1911, disagreement and disquiet about the level of royalty characterized discussion among composers and publishers.

Both these new sources of income had been sought as a result of peacetime changes in the music market. In what ways did the war alter the nature of the market? To start with, some of the major features of the pre-war musical landscape were radically altered by the war. Provincial music festivals were nearly all abandoned, though, with the curtailment of foreign travel, British leisure centres like Harrogate and Brighton benefitted from an influx of visitors and were able to continue to support musical activity, especially orchestras. As a social activity, participation in choral organizations lost support in the war emergency, and the formation of new choirs in munitions manufacturing areas was never really successful due to the strain of long working hours and shift working, which made organization difficult.[1] The popular promenade concerts in the Queen's Hall continued throughout the war, though here, as in many theatres, hotels and restaurants, the shortage of male performers after the introduction of conscription in 1916 opened the way to the employment of women. As befitted a war run initially on *laissez-faire* principles,[2] provision for musical entertainment was left entirely to private initiative. Organizations like Sir Hubert Parry's Music in Wartime Committee and the composer Isidore de Lara's War Emergency Entertainments organization[3] created engagements for professional musicians by arranging concerts in military camps, hospitals, and munitions

1. E. D. Mackerness, *op. cit.*, pp.237–8.
2. A. J. P. Taylor, *English History, 1914–45*, London, 1970, p.64.
3. P. Scholes, *op. cit.*, Vol.II, p.888.

factories. The latter organization was especially important for composers as it specialized in encouraging the performance of new works by British composers, something which professional concert organizers before the war had been strongly criticized for failing to do. Composers of serious music also gained a wider market, albeit temporarily, from the current antipathy towards 'enemy music', though this particular phobia also resulted in the growing popularity of French, Russian and ultimately American musical work.[1] Charitable activities apart, music played its part in the war effort through the 'Recruiting Bands' organization which, in the absence of conscription till 1916, helped speed the volunteers on their way.[2]

Music hall artists did their bit too with prodding songs like 'We don't want to lose you, but we think you ought to go', whilst those who had succumbed to the recruiting song supplied their own war songs from the trenches. 'Tommy's Tunes'[3] were perhaps the first appearance in English music of a genuine popular musical culture unaffected by commercial considerations.[4] Overall, among both combatants and non-combatants war-weariness and the desire to experience immediate and rapid stimulation tended to favour light musical entertainment, especially revues and musical comedy, with much of the material being American in origin.

The release of women from the narrow confines of domestic routine during the war also helped to undermine one other feature of British musical life – the active engagement of large numbers of women in domestic music-making. Before the First World War, the achievement of a degree of musical accomplishment by young women had been regarded as an essential social attribute and had given employment to large numbers of music teachers and composers, who specialized in producing easily-learned adaptations for the piano. This development had,

1. *Ibid.*, p.889.
2. E. D. Mackerness, *op. cit.*, p.239.
3. *Ibid.*, p.240.
4. Though the songs did not lack subsequent commercial exploitation.

however, been closely related to the protected position of young women within middle and upper class Victorian families and to the narrow employment opportunities for women outside the home. War conditions, especially the large scale absorption of women into the war economy, altered the economic and social status of women. Although it is important not to exaggerate the degree of change, as most of the jobs filled by women during the war were promptly vacated by them when peace came, there is little doubt that women were accorded a greater degree of freedom and independence in the 1920s than in the Victorian or Edwardian periods. The decline in the demand for traditional musical skills which followed, was not due to this factor alone. Indeed, in the 1920s, the disappearance of domestic servants probably acted as a force contrary to the liberation of women in the First World War. Precisely that class of woman who would have been adept at the Edwardian musical evening was affected by the emergence of a gap between the disappearance of servants in the 1920s and the availability of labour-saving gadgets in the 1930s. To some extent, therefore, the role of middle-class women tended to be changed into that of the 'housewife' who had less time and energy for domestic music.

A parallel development in the education of women was the rise of domestic science in the 1920s at the expense of some of the more traditional accomplishments. The financial pressures on the public schools and girls' colleges in the 1920s tempted their governing bodies to transfer musical instruction into the category of an optional 'extra', while subjects like domestic science, very useful to a servant-less housewife in the inter-war period, edged their way into the ordinary curriculum. In the smaller establishments full-time teachers of music were replaced by part-time itinerant instructors.

In the 1920s a new range of domestic pastimes developed. Although the gramophone and the wireless brought about the redundancy of the traditional musical skills necessary for domestic entertainment, what the musical evening gave way to was not so much mechanical music, wireless listening or even a visit to the cinema, but a quite different set of activities: cocktail parties, Monopoly, bridge, whist, motor-car excursions, jigsaw puzzles, tennis and (especially in the 1920s) seances! Life in the suburbs, especially in the semi-detached house with its thin party walls demanded peace and quiet from neighbours: pianos and violins were not only wasteful of space, they also made too much noise. The electric gramophone and the wireless had volume knobs and were much more suited to the semi-detached and flat-dwelling middle class of the inter-war years.

The Gramophone

The growth in the popularity of the gramophone and records for music-making both at home and in public increased during the war, and aided the spread of light music. Unlike the infant British film industry, which suffered heavily from wartime restrictions on raw materials and capital expenditure, the British gramophone industry, free from the competition of its main pre-war rivals, Germany and Switzerland, expanded its market and made efforts to raise pre-war standards of reproduction. The mildly eccentric 'phonophile' now became the musically respectable gramophone enthusiast, and by 1921 even the conservative and hostile *Musical Times* allotted a section to record reviews. Another indication of the growing popularity of mechanical music was the foundation, two years later, of a specialized and successful periodical, *The Gramophone*. The contents of the initial issues of this periodical show, however, that in the early 1920s the gramophone had hardly as yet tapped a mass market. Gramophones were still expensive hand-made products. Model changes were frequent and customers were faced with a wide range of optional extras in design. The assumption amongst manufacturers was still that gramophones and records could only be sold to a middle and upper class market. By the end of the decade, as the evidence from the 1928 inquiry into record royalties indicates, manufacturers were well on the way to establishing a mass market for gramophones and records.

How did the commercial outlets for musical entertainment fare during the war? The theatre, the music hall, and especially the new cinema all benefitted from increased wartime demand, partially fed by the rapid growth in wages and salaries. Most important of all, musical entertainment, as a commodity in the leisure market, remained free from rationing and price control, and thereby attracted consumer spending. The significance of this feature of the wartime market can perhaps best be seen in relation to the development of competing demands for consumer expenditure after the war. Even without the intervention of 'mechanical music' many commentators recognized that music was competing in the 1920s and 1930s with other forms of leisure expenditure. The cinema and the wireless, football, motor cycles and cars, gambling and greyhound racing, all enjoyed enormous popularity during the inter-war period. Some of these, especially the first two, opened up new avenues of commercial exploitation, though this was not always recognized by critics, who complained of '. . . a public which has money to spare for everything but the music which it professes to enjoy'.[1] The trouble was that the effects of the new media, cinema and wireless, on the music industry were extremely uneven. This may best be described through developments in the cinema.

The Cinema

A 'technical curiosity' before the war, the cinema developed into 'a fully fledged form of art'[2] by the 1920s. Mute until 1927,[3] the

1. *Musical Times*, December 1933, p.1078.
2. A. J. P. Taylor, *op. cit.*, p.237.
3. It is not entirely correct to say that films were 'mute' until 1927. There were two developments:
   (1) The use of gramophone records which could be synchronized (more or less) with a projector or which were played as background music where the need for precise synchronization could be avoided. An example of the latter is provided by the film, *Poppy*, which also shows the way in which film scores could be exploited by the subsequent sale of gramophone records.
   (2) The second technical development was the *Vitaphone* system. While it is true that the first full-length feature sound film was *The Jazz Singer*, earlier

technical breakthrough which enabled a soundtrack to be synchronized with pictures reconquered the dwindling support for the silent film and established 'the pictures' as 'the essential social habit of the age' during the 1930s. The effect on other forms of entertainment was severe. The music hall was worst hit, but provincial and repertory theatres also suffered badly. Less grand street entertainments such as Punch and Judy, the barrel organ or hurdy gurdy disappeared.[1] Its impact on the musical profession was more complicated. Initially, silent films provided a new outlet for composers and performers alike.[2] As Mackerness has argued, movement without accompanying sound produces an unreal or comic effect,[3] and musical accompaniment was essential to the success of the silent film. The unsuitability of standard classics to fulfil this role left the way open to composers specializing in 'photo-play music . . . for every emotion and incident portrayed on the screen'.[4] Storms, tumults, intrigues, chatter, tragedy, drama, pathos and love – to quote one composer's advertisement – were all given a musical equivalent. Cinema music was not without its critics, but for the musician and composer, as well as the hard pressed publisher, it provided a new form of employment. Cinema pianists, organists and orchestral players all benefitted from the silent film, yet even before the advent of the 'talkie' some loss of employment amongst musical directors in cinemas resulted from the growth of 'special arrangements' to accompany particular films which

the Vitaphone system had been used to provide a partially-synchronized soundtrack. An important example is Warner Brothers' *Don Juan* (1925) which had synchronized sound-effects in its sword play sequences and incidental music provided by the Boston Philharmonic. The quality of the system was insufficient as far as direct transfer to disc was concerned.

1. A. J. P. Taylor, *op. cit.*, pp.392–3.
2. Note: Edwin Evans, distinguished music critic, wrote in 1929 in *Music and Letters* that picture theatres were then providing between three quarters and four fifths of the country's paid musical employment (quoted by Kenneth Young in *Music's Great Days in the Spas and Watering Places*, London, 1968).
3. E. D. Mackerness, *op. cit.*, p.243.
4. Advertisement in *Performing Right*.

were used at a whole circuit of cinemas when the film was shown. However, this loss was small compared with the impact of the 'talkie'.[1] As Ralph Wood wrote in 1939:

... It may be argued that cinema players could never have been an important element in our musical life. In terms of artistic ideals they were indeed not. But they constituted a very large branch of paid performers, and therefore throughout this profession, from composers and publishers to teachers and entrepreneurs, their existence was a factor of weight. The withdrawal of this staple form of musical employment threw the whole system out of balance. Never at all steady, its precariousness now became desperate: and gradual readjustments of supply and demand since have been trifling in comparison with the magnitude of the evil. . . .[2]

Nor was the 'talkie' alone in throwing musicians out of work, for the gramophone now supplied the musical accompaniment that was needed during reel changes and intermissions. For the composer, insofar as he was not engaged in playing, conducting or directing in cinemas, the effect of the 'talkie' was perhaps less serious. Admittedly one sound track replaced a variety of 'situation' compositions, but film music continued to provide an outlet for his talents and although by the late 1930s it could still be said: 'If music be the Cinderella of the Arts, cinema music is one of the Ugly Sisters',[3] film music attracted serious composers such as Richard Addinsell, William Alwyn, Arthur Bliss, Benjamin Britten, John Greenwood and William Walton, and the technical problems of composing for films were being more closely examined.

Apart from the technical problems of this new media, one other feature of the cinema in the inter-war period is worth noticing for its effect on British music. The film industry after

---

1. Another factor which reduced employment opportunities for musicians in cinemas was the increased length of the programme. By the mid-1930s competition between exhibitors was such that double-feature programmes became the rule – even triple – and quadruple-feature programmes. It no longer became necessary to employ live musicians to fill out the length of a cinema programme.
2. R. W. Wood, 'The Future of Music Making', *Musical Times*, February, 1939.
3. A. Benjamin, 'Film Music', *Musical Times*, July 1937.

the First World War was dominated by American interests. Weakened by wartime restrictions, the British film industry faced an industrial competitor who had the advantage of a home market at least four times larger than that of Britain. American film producers could cover their production costs at home and then export at no more than the cost of distribution. With the advent of the 'talkie', the British market was not even protected by language barrier from American films, and the film became an extremely effective vehicle for spreading American cultural tastes and preferences. American films set the popular fashion in hairstyles, clothes and Christian names.[1] Musical tastes were not immune from this as the popularity of the spectacular costume musicals, jazz and song and dance routines testifies. Although like many other home industries in the 1930s, the British film industry received a degree of protection from this competition by means of the Cinematograph Films Act of 1927 (which required renters and distributors to take a compulsory quota of British films), the 'Quota quickies' did little for the reputation of British films. Indeed, it is significant that much of the best film work in this country came from the GPO documentary film unit where public funds were the source of finance and which turned out documentary classics such as Grierson's 'Night Mail' which contained music by Benjamin Britten. Such examples of successful films remain in memory more for their very uniqueness rather than because they were representative of the British film industry's output. For British composers there is little doubt that this weakness of the home film industry was disappointing in the extreme, for in sheer quantitative terms the cinema dominated the mass media in the 1930s. By 1939 when the number of wireless licence holders stood at just over nine million, the average weekly cinema audience was nineteen million.[2]

In feeding the 'appetite for entertainment'[3] the film industry

1. N. Branson & M. Heinemann, *Britain in the 1930s*, London, 1971, pp.251–3.
2. PEP, *The British Film Industry*, London, 1952, p.83.
3. A. Briggs, *The History of Broadcasting in the United Kingdom*, Vol.I, p.6.

was dominated by commercial considerations, both in this country and in the United States. The second of the mass media which grew up in the inter-war period, the wireless, despite exploiting a technology common to both countries, developed along quite different institutional lines in the two countries. In the United States radio was 'integrated into the market complex'[1] and commercial interests from existing media – the press and the cinema – played an important part in shaping it as a means of entertainment. In Britain, broadcasting, despite its foundation in 1922 as a result of the commercial enterprise of the wireless set manufacturers, in 1926 became controlled by a public body, the British Broadcasting Corporation.[2] The content of the new medium was to be non-profit making and the purpose of broadcasting was not seen as a simple provision of entertainment: '. . . I think it will be admitted by all, that to have exploited so great a scientific invention for the purpose and pursuit of entertainment alone would have been a prostitution of its powers and an insult to the character and intelligence of the people . . .'[3]

These two related features of the new medium were of fundamental importance to the music industry in this country and to the public's musical preferences.

Had broadcasting been developed along commercial lines in this country it is likely that entrepreneurs from 'show business' would have played an important part in its establishment and subsequent development. Instead, the initial reaction of the entertainment world to the new medium was one of suspicion, hostility and restriction. Faced by a broadcasting monopoly, the entertainment world itself was forced to combine. In May 1923, a committee of theatre managers, concert promoters, copyright owners, music publishers, composers, artists and stage hands

1. *Ibid.*
2. Between 1922 and 1926 broadcasting was run by the British Broadcasting Company. When a charter was granted in 1926 it became the British Broadcasting Corporation.
3. Lord Reith, quoted in Briggs, *op. cit.*, Vol.I, p.8.

was formed to protect the coalition's interests against the BBC. As far as the groups representing musical interests were concerned, their fear of the BBC was based on much the same ground as their opposition to the gramophone and the cinema: that the new media would provide unwelcome competition to the existing channels by which music reached the public.[1] Asa Briggs, the historian of broadcasting, has criticised this attitude as being '. . . at best timid and at worst obscurantist'[2] in its failure to appreciate the true potential of wireless for opening up a new mass market for entertainment. In view of the depressed state of the theatre, the music hall and the concert world in the face of cinema competition, the restrictive attitude to broadcasting is understandable. Reithian statements concerning the place of music in the new medium such as that music was '. . . the common property and common enjoyment of mankind . . .',[3] whilst pointing to a wider market for music, did little to reassure composers and publishers who had to view their peculiar property rights in a more materialistic manner. Given the loss of income from sheet music suffered by composers and publishers, the inadequate level of gramophone royalties, and the growing opposition of 'music users' – hotels, restaurants, cafes, dance halls, cinemas – to the collection of performing right royalties,[4] there was little sense in acquiescing in the use of music by the BBC without adequately safeguarding copyright property from the outset. Moreover, it was clear in the early days of wireless that the new medium was relying to an unprecedented extent on music of all kinds to supply programme material. As Briggs has said:

Music accounted for by far the biggest slice of broadcasting time. In November 1923, for example, London was broadcasting on an average

1. It may have been an element in these fears that broadcasting was not an act specifically covered by the Copyright Act 1911, so that the legal position was not certain, but in the event broadcasting was interpreted by the Courts as public performance.
2. A. Briggs, *op. cit.*, Vol.I, p.252.
3. Reith quoted in A. Briggs, *op. cit.*, Vol.I, p.244.
4. For the opposition of 'music users' see p.40.

each day 3 hours and 25 minutes of music to 2 hours and 5 minutes of everything else. In 1926 the figures were 4 hours and 40 minutes of music to 2 hours and 20 minutes of everything else.[1]

In view of the rapid growth of wireless licences (see table 3.1), over two million by 1926, it was clear that the competition offered by the new medium was of an unprecedented nature and this merely accentuated the necessity of forming a satisfactory arrangement for the use of copyright material from the start.

Table 3.1

Year (31 December)	Number of wireless licences
1922	35,744
1923	595,496
1924	1,129,578
1925	1,645,207
1926	2,178,259

Source: Based on A. Briggs, op. cit., Vol.I, p.18.

On the other hand, to view the possibilities of broadcasting simply from an economic standpoint, important as it was to composers, was indeed to neglect the other benefits which the wireless might hold for music. The appointment of a Musical Advisory Committee in 1925 and an Advisory Committee on Opera in 1926 by the BBC pointed the way to the role of broadcasting in improving musical taste among a growing audience. Financial patronage of the near bankrupt British National Opera Company from 1923 and the successful salvaging of the Queen's Hall Promenade Concerts in 1927 – incidentally overcoming William Boosey's deeply held belief that broadcasting would ruin the concert world – confirmed the seriousness with which the BBC interpreted its responsibility to music and also reflected the changing public taste in music as a result of the wireless. From the point of view of professional musicians, the BBC had one other feature greatly to its credit. Although gramophone records were used as early as 1922, the BBC, unlike American

1. A. Briggs, *op. cit.*, Vol.I, p.275.

Sir William Boosey,
founder member of the
Performing Right Society

Sir Edward German,
the British composer who
strongly supported the Per-
forming Right Society in the
1920s

A. P. Herbert, one of the earliest opponents of the 'Tuppenny Bill' – in a contemporary photograph

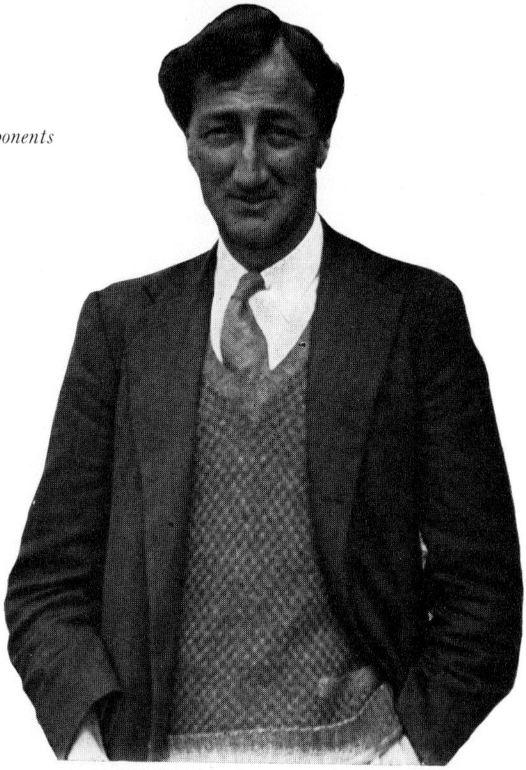

David Low's famous cartoon

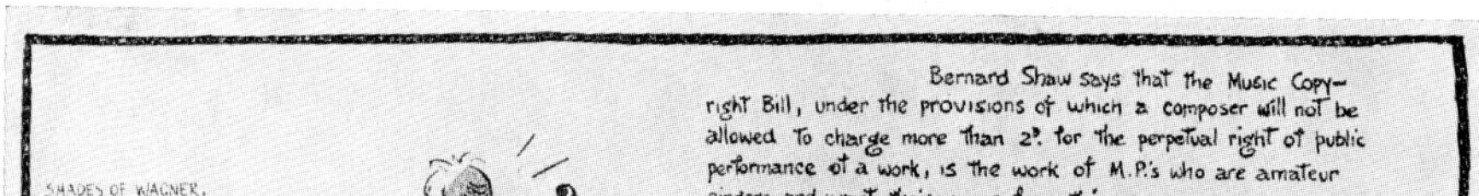

TUPPENCE !

From the *Evening Standard*] [*By kind permission*

broadcasting companies, did not rely on them as a low-cost substitute for live performers. Instead, it developed its own dance
bands and orchestras which gave employment to professional
musicians at a time when alternative employment opportunities
were shrinking. In the light of the subsequent continuation of the
BBC's music policy in the 1930s in the creation of the BBC Symphony Orchestra; in its emphasis on quality; in its work in
musical education and in opera, all of which gave serious music
a greater outlet than a commercial institution would have done,
or indeed was probably warranted on a narrower interpretation
of the public's existing preferences, it is hard, in retrospect, to
understand the persistent sniping of serious music critics,
'against the predominance of bad music, the jazzing and guying
of the classics; the detestable croonings, "harmonizings" and
other vulgarities in vaudeville and dance items; the undue pro-
minance given to cinema organs and restaurant bands . . .'[1]
What this criticism probably reflected was a growing awareness
by composers, publishers and performing musicians that access
to the 'air' was as crucial for commercial success as had been
access to the concert hall in the nineteenth century. At the
serious end of the music market this awareness tended to show
itself in criticism of the space given to all 'low brow' music, in a
desire for protection against works by foreign composers, and
perhaps saddest of all, in a preference for familiar and well-tried
works at the expense of new compositions. With light music,
the struggle for access to the new medium resulted in an increase
in the practice of 'plugging' songs. Plugging had existed in the
music market long before the appearance of broadcasting, and
special payments to singers and musical directors by publishers
and writers had long been a recognized means of ensuring public
performance of new works.[2] Faced with a broadcasting monopoly, the only means of directly influencing the content of music
programmes was for the publisher or song writer to pay dance

1. *Musical Times*, April 1933.
2. The meaning of song plugging has changed in the last forty years. Whilst
plugging has always involved special payments, it was also, until about 1930,

band leaders for playing selected items. Those who were unable to make such payments were simply left out.[1] To satisfy the large number of complaints about plugging, the BBC prohibited dance band leaders from using announcing microphones.[2] This drastic solution left the public bemused and offered no long term solution to the problem. Despite the appointment, in 1933, of a special BBC official who had the power to ban offenders from the air for at least six months, the problem remained and was still an active source of irritation between songwriters and the BBC after the Second World War.

In 1925 the Crawford Committee was set up to examine the future of broadcasting. The music publishers maintained in evidence that broadcasting had harmfully affected the sale of sheet music; it had cut down the life of a popular song from twelve months to less than six months; it had led to fewer concerts; it had destroyed the amateur performer and was in the process of pushing the professional musician out of older markets such as hotels and restaurants. By 1939, when there were 9·08 million licence holders compared with 2·17 million in 1926, it was clear that many of these early fears about the impact of broadcasting had been allayed. In fact it is difficult to believe that these supposed effects were not due to other fundamental causes. Even before broadcasting the gramophone had cut the life of popular songs, and for publishers to complain about what really amounted to an increase in turnover was an odd reflection on their business initiative. The public concert had been in decline as far back as the Edwardian period, and even allowing

---

regarded as a legitimate form of advertisement in the music trade and a 'song-plugger' was simply a man who played the piano in large music shops for the benefit of purchasers of sheet music.

1. Somewhat later the PRS felt obliged to resort to the exclusion from its distribution plan of arrangers of copyright (as distinct from non-copyright) works because of the practice by band leaders of demanding special arrangements for their orchestras, the arranger being either the band leader himself or someone nominated by him.

2. A. Briggs, *op. cit.*, Vol.II, p.86.

for this there was some evidence to suggest that the BBC had given public concerts a new audience and a fresh lease of life. As the Editor of the *Musical Times* wrote in 1928:

'. . . It may well prove . . . that the BBC, so far from killing the public concert, will give it a new lease of life. Its concerts at Queen's Hall have clearly tapped a fresh public. At each concert I have found myself surrounded by refreshingly unsophisticated folk. Evidently they had heard orchestras at home, and had decided to go and see one – for they took in almost as much pleasure through the eye as through the ear. At first one thought these hearers were Promenaders who had stolen back to their old haunt, but clearly they were quite new hands . . .'[1]

That the audience should have been composed of 'refreshingly unsophisticated folk' not only revealed how 'un-public' the old style public concert had been with its predominantly middle and upper class audience but also suggests that its ossification in a rapidly changing society was another reason for its decline. Another feature of the BBC's music policy which met with approval from some critics was: 'its valuable salvage work. Hardly a week passes without the performance of several compositions that in the ordinary way would never be heard in public . . .'[2] An extended market, and extended repertoire – these were the BBC's greatest contribution to music in the inter-war period. Freed from the pressures of commercial criteria, musical taste was able to revise its preferences.[3] The problem for the composer however was not merely that of adjusting his work to suit the changed demand but also to ensure that he was adequately remunerated for its use in this new market.

Before examining the arrangements made by composers and publishers, two other innovations may be mentioned at this point. The first followed directly from wireless. This was the sizeable growth of 're-diffusion' services by wireless exchange to subscribers. Although the number of subscribers (over

1. P. Scholes, *op. cit.*, Vol.II, p.797.
2. *Ibid.*
3. E. D. Mackerness, *op. cit.*, p.256.

200,000 by 1935) was but a fraction of the number of wireless licence holders, the new service raised interesting problems. It faced the BBC with competition which often involved the relay of output from foreign commercial stations such as Radio Luxembourg and Radio Normandie and raised questions of copyright both in the use of BBC output and in the composer's original copyright. The second innovation, television, really only rose to importance as one of the mass media in the 1950s, but it is worth remembering that television broadcasting began in 1936 and that by 1939 (when the service was closed down on the outbreak of war) between twenty and twenty-five thousand sets were in use. Unlike the wireless, there was less hesitancy on the part of composers and publishers alike to allow copyright material to be used in programmes, though impresarios and artists did oppose the new medium because of fear about its likely effect on existing channels of entertainment. The more conciliatory attitude of copyright owners was probably due to the relatively satisfactory arrangements which had been made with the BBC for the use of copyright material in broadcasting. Also, it was felt that television could never seriously rival radio for home entertainment because, in addition to the high cost of receiving apparatus, mass production of original material for television broadcasting would be too costly.

Thus, in the inter-war years, the spread of three important innovations, the gramophone, the cinema and the wireless radically altered the nature of the music market. What some described as the industrialization of music[1] had taken place at last, but to see these developments simply as the application of new techniques of communication to a mass market is to ignore a large part of the interesting social changes which occurred alongside them. The spread of American culture in jazz music and the cinema, the dance craze of the 1920s, and the 'listening habit' of the wireless audience all reflected marked changes in social behaviour. Above all, the ubiquitous wireless opened up a new audience for music, and even in the depths of the depression

1. L. Sabaneev, 'Music and the Economic Crisis', *Musical Times*, December 1934.

in 1929 to 1933 the number of licences doubled. Unlike other channels for music where expenditure was reduced, the wireless gave not merely stability but growth to the market. Although for some musicians – the modern 'Bolton weavers' – the new media amounted to an 'economic and technical pogrom'[1] for others 'the inquiry for music . . . from the great unmusical class' opened up new sources of income.

The Performing Right 1914–39

Until this Society was formed in 1914, chaos reigned supreme: unless under specifically defined contracts, the average musician received no fee for performing rights in his works. His brain was a sort of No-Man's-Land on which every predatory spirit squatted to work it dry for his (the pirate's) not the producer's profit.[2]

Although rescued from No-Man's-Land by the legal protection granted in the 1911 Copyright Act and by the formation of the Performing Right Society in 1914, chaos was not transformed into order overnight. The problems arising from the attempt to establish another source of income for the composer in the face of the rapid technological changes occurring in the music market were complex and cut across many traditional contractual relationships in the music industry. It is the aim of this section to establish the nature of these problems and the manner in which solutions to them were sought.

The creation of the Performing Right Society, whilst a considerable diplomatic achievement in view of the heterogeneous interests in the sheet music market, did not guarantee an end to the struggle to assert the performing right. What it did do, however, was to give composers, lyric authors and publishers an organization through which to defend their interests, and the subsequent growth in income from performing right royalties can be examined as much through the history of the institution as through the economic circumstances of the music industry.

1. L. Sabaneev, *op. cit.*   2. *The PR Gazette*, 1923.

For example, the bitter dispute between the Society and the Musicians' Union in the early 1920s sprang not solely from a direct clash of economic interests – the fear that performance royalties based on the number of musicians employed would limit the amount of money spent on musicians – but also from the personal animosity of the leading personality in each organization.[1] In view of the limited scope of the present study such factors will not be examined except where they appear to have been of overwhelming importance in determining the policy of the Performing Right Society.

Before examining the problems associated with the collection of performing right royalties some statistics on the growth of the Society's activities may provide a useful background to the discussion. In the period from 1914 to 1939 the steady upward trend is marked by two distinct periods of rapid growth, 1925–26 and 1934–8. In only one year, 1919–20, did membership actually decline, and then only by a very small number. The decrease in 1919–20 is explained by the resignation of about fifty members who were publishers of 'popular' music, and the composers and authors who were associated with them. These publishers of popular music came from the new firms which were established after the First World War to meet the demand for dance numbers in sheet music form.[2] Centred in the Charing Cross Road area of London, the new home of the light music industry, their secession was partly the result of their continuing belief that sales of sheet music could provide an adequate return for the publisher, and partly the results of pressure from the Musicians' Union. Despite tapping a demand for a new sort of music, these publishers adopted an attitude to the collection of performing right royalties which had much in common with the nineteenth-century arrangements for popularizing sheet music.

1. William Boosey, President of the P R S and J. B. Williams, Secretary of the Musicians' Union. Two quotes by Boosey give the flavour of their dispute; on Williams: 'Where composers' performing rights are concerned Mr Williams' views are Bolshevistic.' On the Union: 'These gentlemen who are the spoilt darlings of the musical profession.'
2. E. D. Mackerness, *op. cit.*, p.251.

They believed that free permisssion for performance constituted an advertisement of such worth as to compensate for the loss of performance royalties. With the spread of cheap gramophone records and the development of broadcasting from 1922, the fallacy of the 'free music' argument was rapidly exposed, and by the time of their renewal of membership in 1926 these publishers had been forced into seeking payment for the use of their material in broadcasting. The pressure on them from the Musicians' Union was of a different nature. It took the form of a threatened boycott of their music. Although the boycott never got beyond being a threat,[1] the attitude of the Musicians' Union is worth considering as it was a tactic adopted by other music users later in the 1920s. As has been discussed above,[2] one feature of the music market prior to the First World War had been the payments made by publishers and composers to singers, directors, conductors and musicians for the use of the publisher's music. With the collection of performing right royalties and the dwindling returns from sheet music, the publishers refused to make these payments. This constituted one part of the Union's grievance against the Society. The other part originated from an unfortunate early decision on the basis of tariff charges by the Society. As will be discussed below, the basis on which fees are calculated was, and remains, a complex and difficult problem. A proposal in 1918 to base tariffs on the number of musicians employed by the music user seemed to pose a direct threat to the employment of musicians.[3] Although the Society quickly dropped this form of tariff, the Union's action highlighted the conflict of interest between the publisher, composer and executant which the new contractual arrangements produced.

With the return of the popular music publishers to the Society in 1926, membership increased by 291 in that year and by 1930

---

1. There were, however, strikes by musicians when they were asked to play material in the P R S repertoire. See the Special Report from the Select Committee on the Musical Copyright Bill (1930) at questions 787, 813–17. Hereafter cited as Special Report (etc.) (1930).
2. See pp.40ff.
3. Special Report (etc.) (1930), at questions 787, 813–17.

the original membership of 39 in 1914 had reached 1,015. Yet even growth on this scale, whilst giving the Society a majority of the repertoire of British music, still left the Society incomplete in its representation. Although it could be claimed that: '. . . the publication of music bearing the words "may be performed in public without fee or licence" has almost entirely ceased . . . "Free Music" has been discarded'[1]; and though it was true that the success of a musical item was no longer to be judged on sheet music sales alone but also on its generation of performing right royalties, there still remained a sizeable minority of publishers outside the Society. This group,[2] led by Novello, had catalogues consisting mainly of educational and sacred music and their markets had been less affected by 'mechanical music'. The attitude of this group towards the collection of performance royalties is best seen in the following statement by Novello in 1929. It is taken from a leader[3] opposing the licensing arrangements made by the Society with religious bodies for the use of music in secular entertainments: 'As the chief object of the publication of music is to ensure performance, it does not seem reasonable to tax the performer for doing the very thing the publisher wants him to do. Messrs Novello therefore do not belong to the Performing Right Society.'

Novello in fact were still adhering to the old principle of using the performing right as a means of defence against performances from borrowed, second-hand or hired copies, though it is interesting to note that free performances were not extended by Novello to the use of their material in broadcasting, a sure sign that broadcasting was affecting their market. Even excluding losses on sheet music sales, solo negotiations with the BBC and other music users meant that these publishers were bearing unenviably high transaction costs, and in 1936 Novello announced that they had joined the Society for the following reasons:

1. *The PR Gazette*, 1926.
2. Stainer & Bell Ltd and the Oxford University Press were also in this group.
3. *Musical Times*, 1 December 1929, p.1073.

'Music of all kinds, including the best, is now used in a great number of places, and for a variety of purposes, that would have been considered unlikely a decade or so ago. As some of these developments (e.g. that of music for film purposes) are clearly destined to become widespread, it is manifestly impossible for the interests of publishers and composers to be protected under the individual system that was formerly adequate. Moreover, collection of fees for performance in foreign countries is more effectively done by the P R S in concert with similar foreign bodies. Composers who have in print any substantial number of works will be well advised to follow the example of the publishers and join the Society.'[1]

Their recommendation induced many others to follow suit and between 1935 and 1939 membership of the Society increased from 1,374 to 1,861. With the accession of this publishing group: '. . . recognition of the principle of the collection of performing right fees through a central organization became unanimous'.[2]

Important as this now united front became, recognition of the principle of the collection of performance royalties was still not universal amongst music users. Undoubtedly the most important of the Society's early tasks was simply that of persuading music users to pay for something that had been generally regarded as a free good.[3] It was no easy task in view of the strength of the commercial interests involved in the entertainment world. Despite the fact that as early as 1914 some of the most important providers of musical entertainment such as Moss Empires, the Alhambra and Stoll Music Halls, J. Lyons & Co. Ltd, the Savoy, Berkeley and Claridge's Hotels, and several municipal corporations had taken out licences, a large body of music users refused to recognize the public performing right and remained implacably opposed to the principle of collection. This opposition generally took one of two forms. At the level of the

1. *Ibid.*, January 1936.   2. C. F. James, *op. cit.*, p.79.
3. This statement does not of course apply to operas and dramatic musical works where performance royalties were easier to collect because of the length and infrequent performance of the work.

individual dance hall owner, cinema owner or publican it simply consisted of denying the right and refusing to pay a licence fee. As such it served more as a time-wasting irritant and was usually dealt with by a lawyer's letter or, if that failed, by legal action for infringement. Whilst until the late 1920s every attempt to collect a licence royalty carried with it a potential legal action, such intransigent individuals were but a fact of everyday business and posed no serious threat to the Society. Much more worrying was the appearance of organized opposition amongst music users to the Society's activities. Although the Society established the principle of negotiating contracts with representative trade associations such as the Theatrical Managers' Association, the Cinematograph Exhibitors' Association, and the Showmen's Guild, right from the outset, it was not a policy free from risk. Composers and publishers having united to assert their rights, it was just as likely that music users would group together to protect their own interests. So long as the aims of these Associations were simply to increase their members' bargaining power with the PRS and to lessen the transactions costs of individual negotiations, their activities from the PRS point of view were both legitimate and helpful, for they facilitated the collection of royalties.

The appearance of the British Music Union Ltd in 1919 marked opposition to the Society of a different nature. Its line of attack was to publish a catalogue of 'free music', that is music which was either out of copyright or for which the publisher did not assert the performing right. The most effective countermove against this attack was to ensure that the membership, and hence the repertoire, of the Society grew as fast as possible; besides the growth in British membership, the contracts of affiliation with foreign societies, whose national repertoires were also covered by the PRS licence charge, worked to this end. Less easily dealt with, however, was the attempt by the British Music Union in 1923 and 1924 to weaken the Copyright Act of 1911 by promoting an amending Bill in Parliament. Both these failed, but in 1927 a new and more comprehensive association of music users, the International Council of Music Users Ltd, was formed. Its membership[1] covered a large number of proprietors of hotels, restaurants, cafés, clubs, dance halls, public halls, as well as gramophone companies, corporations, cinemas, the National Operatic and Dramatic Association, the National Chamber of Trade, the Music Trades Association and the Musicians' Union. Although its aims were to defend its members against the actions of the Performing Right Society and to endeavour: 'to provide that the charges made to its members for the performance of music in public shall be upon a fair and more equitable basis',[2] its actions, after its attempt to secure bulk discounts on tariffs failed, took the form of a renewed attempt to weaken the 1911 Copyright Act. Under the 1911 Act, the composer enjoyed as part of his copyright the sole right to perform his work in public, and to decide upon what terms his work might be performed in public by any other person. These rights were not subject to any conditions or restrictions. The Musical Copyright Bill which was promoted by the International Council of Music Users proposed two amendments to the 1911 Act. The first intended to make it compulsory to print a notice reserving the performing right on every copy of the work as a condition of the retention of the performing right. The second amendment struck directly at the composer's right to set the terms on which he would dispose of his right to another. It involved the principle of a compulsory licence in respect of performing rights – where they had been retained by printing the required notice – with a fixed maximum royalty of 2d which the owner might demand from the music user. The fee was to cover the performance right in perpetuity of any musical work, irrespective of the extent or nature of the work or the size, nature or character of the place of performance. It was this provision which gave the bill its nickname of 'The Tuppenny Bill' and also inspired a famous cartoon by David Low. Apart from the restriction on the composer's rights which the bill involved, in

1. Special Report (etc.) (1930), at question 461.
2. C. F. James, *op. cit.*, p.52.

direct contravention to Britain's adherence to the Berne Convention of 1908, the appealing simplicity of the twopenny royalty ignored many of the changes which had made reliance on the sale of sheet music untenable.

By 1930 it was only too clear that the sale of sheet music was not commensurate with the increased demand for music. The bill would, for example, have enabled the BBC to entertain its millions of listeners for the price of a single copy of sheet music, instead of the £60,000 which broadcasting royalties were bringing to the PRS in 1930. The proposed bill produced a wave of opposition. One of the earliest opponents was A. P. Herbert who pointed to the inequitable remuneration between creator and executant:

'A very well-known London hotel paid last year £33,318 to its three orchestras and £186 to the PRS as composers' fees. Another paid £36,745 to its orchestras and £153 to the PRS for the composers. So of the total music bill for these rich hotels about half of 1 per cent was "exacted" by this vampire body for the composer, the creator, and 99½ per cent went to the executant, the mere interpreter, the saxophonist. But nothing was said in the House of Commons about limiting the remuneration of orchestras, and no one ventured to describe the Musicians' Union as a wart or vampire.'

In sum, 'The Tuppenny Bill' was: 'the most unjust, unprincipled, muddle-headed, ill-drafted, unworkable measure that was ever printed by His Majesty's printers.'[1] Such a superb denunciation should not, however, obscure the fact that the bill synthesized many of the genuine fears of music users about the role under the 1911 Act of the Performing Right Society.

The two main complaints made by music users against the Society were:

1   that the Society did not publish any list of the works controlled and therefore it was impossible for the music user to discover what music was controlled by the Society's licence and what was not; and

1. *Punch*, 4 December 1929.

2 that the Society had made arbitrary increases in the licence
   fees and that music users had no means of protecting themselves against further increases, or of ensuring any reasonable stability in the charges.

As far as the first complaint was concerned, the refusal of the
PRS to publish a catalogue was partly due to the administrative
duties and costs involved – until the mid-1920s administrative
costs absorbed between a third and a half of the Society's income
– and partly to the fear that perfect knowledge on the part of the
music user about what was, and what was not, copyright would
aid the 'free music' campaign. By 1930, although the absolute
costs of administration were higher, the percentage of gross
income absorbed had fallen to around 17 per cent and the Society
could afford to adopt a more generous approach to this request.
Also, so long as the 1911 Act remained in force, the increasing
membership and repertoire of the Society meant that the 'free
music' campaign offered diminishing danger to the Society. As a
result the Society offered to circulate to all its licensees a complete list of all its publisher members which substantially met the
difficulties music users had in determining the existence of copyright in music they wished to use. The need to do this did not
last long for it soon became evident that the Society's system of
licensing held substantial advantages for music users in relation
to their liabilities under the 1911 Copyright Act.

The system of licensing adopted by the Society, and generally
by all other similar societies which now exist in nearly every
advanced country, is to issue blanket licences to perform any and
every work in its repertoire for a specific period, usually one
year, the licence being automatically renewed at the end of this
period unless cancelled. The licence is issued to the proprietors
or responsible managers of the premises where music is performed in public, and not to the performers as such, although
they are the persons actually giving the performance. Thus the
music user clears the public performance right in what is now
virtually the world repertoire of copyright music under a single

contract for a single annual payment. The performance of a single work or group of works on one or more specific occasions can also be licensed.

The advantages of this system to the performers and large-scale users, from the broadcasters downward, were soon recognized. The artist was free to choose among the world's repertoire whatever works he wished to perform without worrying about his legal liability under the Copyright Act, the P R S having covered his liability for him. The music user had the same advantage, together with the enormous economies resulting from a single package deal with, effectively, the copyright owners of the whole world.

The music users' first complaint was relatively easy to solve. Their second grievance was more tendentious and less easily handled, for it arose from the very nature of the organization needed to protect copyright property. A Special Select Committee of the House of Commons, to whom the Musical Copyright Bill was referred, expressed the problem in their report as follows:

Your Committee are agreed that a fixed fee cannot be applied to all the varying circumstances of public performance if the composer is to receive a reasonable remuneration. Nor do they wish to place any obstacle in the way of composers forming an association for the purposes of protection and enforcing their rights. Such an Association is undoubtedly a convenience and almost a necessity, both to the composer, the music publisher and the user of music, who would be considerably embarrassed if he had to deal separately with each piece of music performed. In fact, it may be said to be the only practicable way in which the composer can collect his fees for such performing rights in an adequate manner. If such an undertaking is to function effectively it must obtain as nearly as possible a super-monopoly of the monopolies conferred upon composers by the Copyright Act. Your Committee consider that such a supermonopoly can abuse its rights by refusing to grant licences upon reasonable terms so as to prejudice the trade or industry of persons carrying on business in this country and to be contrary to the public interest, and that it should be open to those persons to obtain relief in respect of such abuse by appeal to arbitration or some other tribunal. This should apply only in those cases where the ownership or control of copyright has been transferred to an association.

'A super-monopoly of monopolies – this was exactly the basis of the problem in tariff negotiation as the music users saw it. For the PRS to operate effectively, it needed the greatest possible ability to afford the music user protection against infringement of the public performing right, but with it the Society's every action was open to the easy accusation of monopoly abuse.[1] What had heightened the fears of even friendly music users like Mr Walter Payne, Chairman of the Entertainments Protection Association (who said that his Association did not 'seek to avoid payment of any reasonable fee for the performance of music, nor to deprive composers or authors of their livelihood . . .'),[2] had been the revision and increase of tariffs from 1926. With the accession to membership of the popular music publishers in 1926 the Society had been faced with the 'necessity of revising present fees in order to provide revenue for new members without diminishing that of older members'.[3] The problem was not confined to the increased membership from British sources alone. In addition to the repertoire of copyright music vested in the Society by its own members, the Society also represented the repertoires of similar foreign societies through its contracts of affiliation with them. By 1930 approximately 26,000[4] foreign composers, authors and music publishers were represented by the PRS and their copyright works covered by PRS licences. To maintain the existing level of distributions to members it was essential for the PRS to increase its tariffs. Here then was the crux of the problem for the Society. Welcome as the increase in membership in 1926 (and later in 1936) had been with its attendant recognition of the performing right, it posed the problem of the upward re-

1. Although the Society could be described as possessing a monopoly of copyright music there is in existence a vast public domain of music which has fallen out of copyright at the end of the protection period specified by the Act. In the serious music field this provides fierce competition for the contemporary composer.
2. Special Report (etc.) (1930) at question 906.
3. *The PR Gazette*, 1936.
4. Special Report (etc.) (1930) at question 1,428.

vision in the Society's tariffs, which automatically confirmed the worst fears and suspicions of the music users. To the music user perhaps drawing on only a very small part of the P R s repertoire, arguments about the invaluable worth of the entire repertoire seemed invalid, even though the tariffs were adjusted to the scale of use, and it was argued that 'the intrinsic value of the music contracted for was and is unknown, and its proper value remains entirely a matter of speculation'.[1]

To the Society's members, on the other hand, witnessing the rapid growth of demand for music in dance halls, jazz clubs, cinemas and broadcasting, the commercial value of their product seemed self evident, and at least not unsubstantial.

While it is easy to appreciate the problem which the Select Committee had to meet, it is difficult to describe its recommendation – a tribunal of arbitration – as being in any sense a meaningful solution, for it did nothing to solve the fundamental difficulty of determining the criteria by which a solution acceptable to either party could be reached. Moreover, the proposal was contrary to the terms of the Berlin Copyright Convention of 1908, and the Board of Trade was given the task of framing a policy for adoption at the next meeting of the Berne Copyright Union 'which would secure freedom for His Majesty's Government to deal with any abuse of monopoly rights . . .'.[2] In these words lay the seeds from which the Performing Right Tribunal was to spring. The Berne Copyright Union was scheduled to meet in 1935. With the international troubles of the 1930s and the Second World War the Convention was not, in fact, revised until 1948. For over a quarter of a century the P R s was to operate in the shadow of an impending supervisory body. Much more immediately satisfying for the Society was that in July 1930 the 'Tuppenny Bill', the source of all this mischief, was reported by the Select Committee without amendment, which meant that it could not be proceeded with.

Whilst the International Council of Music Users was a combination of consumers, it at no time reached a position where it

1. *Ibid.*, at question 768.   2. *Ibid.*, at p.vi.

Varaldi's Savoy Tango Band, 1925, one of the famous bands of the period

A Wurlitzer Console cinema organ of the 1930s

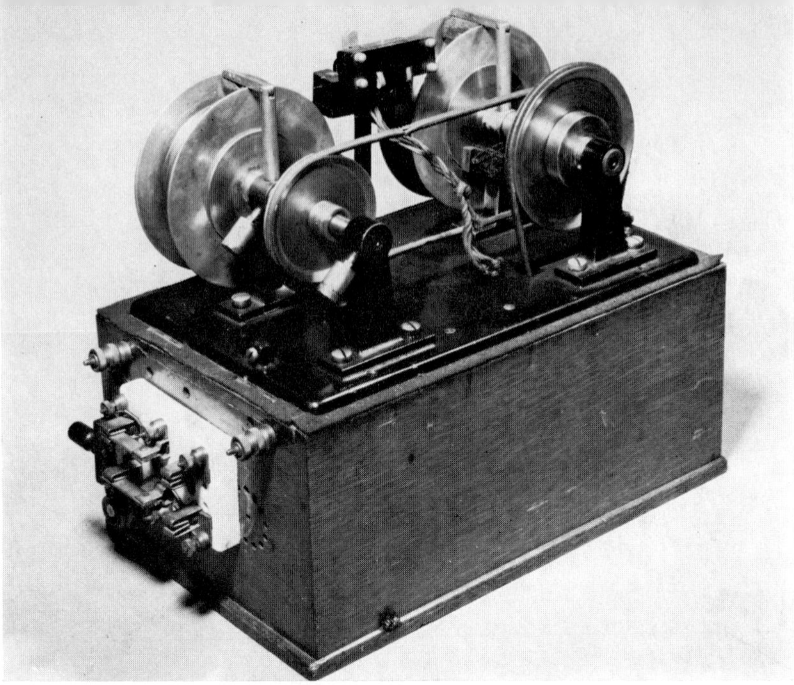

The magnetic tape recorder, 1899, invented by Poulsen

Messrs. Parkins and Gotto, of 60, Oxford Street, have provided a surprisingly clever and amusing toy for the Christmas holidays—the Gramophone, or Speaking Machine. Imagine the surprise of the little ones, and even of their elders—not unfamiliar with the mysteries of the phonograph—when the Gramophone steadily recites "Old Mother Hubbard," and this without the least preparation or special skill on the part of the manipulator! We slip off one disc and replace it with another, turn the handle again, and one hears "Twinkle, Twinkle. Little Star," "Sing a Song of Sixpence," "Who Killed

THE GRAMOPHONE, OR SPEAKING MACHINE.

Cock Robin?" or—for the Gramophone is thoroughly cosmopolitan—"Deutschland, Deutschland, über Alles!" A toy at once so clever, so mirth-giving, and at the same time so simple, we have not seen for many a day.

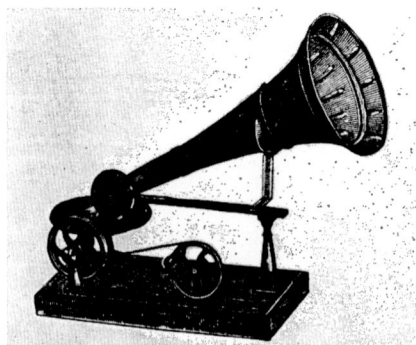

A phonograph advertisement from the Illustrated London News

could offer a united front in negotiations with the PRS. The various channels of musical communication – theatres (for non-dramatic performances), restaurants, cinema – could all be licensed separately by the Society. In this case there existed no element of monopoly on the purchasing side. The case of wireless was quite different. Here the PRS faced in tariff negotiations a monopsonist, that is, a sole buyer, access to the medium of radio being controlled by the British Broadcasting Corporation. The qualitative importance of this new medium in the inter-war years has already been discussed.[1] 'Nowadays the majority of our citizens are listeners rather than performers'[2] declared the *Gazette* in 1932, and by far the biggest concentration of listeners was to be reached through the wireless. Securing a return to the composer for the use of his music in this medium was vitally important, for by 1930 35 per cent of the Society's income came from this source. Fifteen years later almost half the Society's domestic income arose from broadcasting royalties, to make radio the biggest single market and the fastest growing down to 1945. Apart from the absence of normal commercial criteria by

Table 3.2   *Income from B B C 1929 and 1936*

Year	No. of licences	Amount paid by BBC	Empire Service
1929	2,614,324	£45,000	n.a.
1936	7,359,327	£121,926	£6,300
New Agreement estimates:			
1937	8,000,000	£233,000	£23,000

Source: *The PR Gazette*, 1937.   n.a.: not applicable.

which the BBC could judge the value of musical composition to itself, the income of the BBC was uncertain, and influenced by government subvention.[3] As a result of the latter, the Society in 1932 was required by the Corporation to bear a proportion of the Corporation's special contribution to the Treasury. From

1. See pp.62–9.   2. *The PR Gazette*, 1932.
3. By the Post Office to cover costs of collecting licence money and by the Treasury for general budgetary reasons.

1929 the B B C's payments to the Society were based on the number of listeners' licences issued, up to a limit of 5 per cent of the B B C's share of the licence revenue: a limitation which operated to the Society's disadvantage at a time when licences were growing very rapidly. The adoption of a sliding scale charge[1] matched the principle behind the B B C's share and with the dropping of the 5 per cent limit resulted, as can be seen from table 3.2, in a substantial growth in broadcasting income during the periods of the agreement.

*

Substantial as was the increase in income under the 1929 and 1938 agreements, it was found that the extent of the B B C's use of the Society's repertoire had increased at a faster rate, with the result that the amount distributable per work, instead of showing an improvement, in fact decreased, indicating that a payment method based on the number of listeners' licences was unsatisfactory unless it was also associated with any increase in the extent of the use made in the P R S repertoire. Two other factors also came into consideration in the proposals the Society made for a new agreement with the B B C in 1937 – the growing belief that the decline in composers' royalties from the sale of sheet music and gramophone records was largely attributable to broadcasting, and the knowledge that the B B C under its new Charter (covering the period 1937–47) would receive a larger share of the listeners' licence fee.[2] All these factors distilled into a claim for payment of 1s 0d per licence, subject to a proportionate increase in the event of any increase in the number of hours of broadcasting during the agreement.[3] Against this, the B B C offered a payment of 5d per licence and said it was not prepared to enter into any negotiations for an increase in its offer.

1. Under 1933 agreement: on first 1 million licences, 5¼d per licence; on second million licences, 4½d per licence; on third million licences, 3½d per licence; in excess of 3 million 3¼d per licence.
2. Six-tenths out of the licence fee of 10s. The balance went to the Post Office and the Treasury.
3. A claim to cover the use of P R S material in the Empire Service was also made.

A monopsonist deadlocked with a monopolist suggested only one remedy: that the dispute be referred to voluntary arbitration. This was in fact to be the only case of arbitration over PRS licence fees before the Second World War. It proved to be an expensive and time-consuming method of solving tariff disputes but at least in this case the result of the tribunal's deliberations was favourable – an award of 7d per licence for home broadcasting.[1] The overall effect of the award was to double the payment previously received by the Society.

These negotiations with the BBC have been covered at length not because they were typical of tariff negotiations at this time but rather because they were atypical. The wireless audience was the composer's largest pre-war market. Both qualitatively and quantitatively the wireless was all-pervasive. In no other market did the PRS face a monopsonist; nor was there any other organization in this country with which the Society had to deal which was so dependent on government policy decisions for determining the size of its income.

One other aspect of the relationship between the PRS and the BBC is worth considering at this point. This was the attempt by some members of the PRS to use the Society's licence as a means of influencing the music policy of the BBC. From its foundation the PRS issued licences without attaching conditions to the type or origin of the music that the user might have. The licence covered the whole of the Society's repertoire and the user was free to select any item from it. The importance of this principle of free choice was that it enabled the PRS, as a collecting society, to discharge both domestic and international responsibilities. Thus the PRS could not discriminate against foreign composers, neither could a foreign society favour its own nationals. The obligation of non-discrimination was a fundamental contractual condition governing the reciprocal relations between performance right licensing societies and from its inception the PRS steadfastly refused to be drawn into policies which would dis-

1. One tenth of the amount payable for home stations for the use of material in the Empire Service.

criminate between British and foreign composers. This stand, however, still left open another question: whether the licensing power might be used to secure ends other than the protection of copyright and the collection of royalties. The issue which provoked an attempt by some PRS members to impose conditions on the BBC through the PRS licence was the troublesome question of 'plugging' on the wireless. As previously discussed,[1] the BBC banned conductors from the microphone to prevent this advertising element in the 1920s. The PRS became involved in this matter when it came to negotiate the 1929 licensing agreement. With the re-accession of the popular publishers in 1926 the internal political balance of the PRS swung in favour of these publishers, and they exercised pressure on the Society to make it a condition of the licence agreement that the announcing ban be dropped. Given the BBC's peculiar constitutional position it could only resist any attempt to dictate the manner of programme presentation. On the grounds of public policy the BBC was not merely prepared to take legal action but was also intending to apply to the Board of Trade for a tribunal to investigate the dispute. Fortunately, in view of the likely unfavourable light in which this would have cast the PRS contractual powers, the issue was never examined in public. The ban on plugging was dropped, partly because of public pressure, and a verbal assurance to the PRS that it would not be re-imposed resulted in the Society's licence being issued. This assurance enabled Leslie Boosey, the then Chairman of the PRS, to secure the popular music publishers' support for the licensing agreement.[2] Such an attempt to use the Society's monopoly powers as a vehicle for other ends did not again rise in the 1930s, and by 1947 the popular composers and lyric-writers created the Songwriters' Guild, an organization more suited to waging such campaigns, because it was free of obligations towards equivalent foreign associations. This, like the earlier organization for the serious composer, the Composers' Guild (founded 1944) set about the task of attempting to influence the BBC's music policy after the Second World War.

1. See p.31.   2. Special Report (etc.) (1930), Appendix XI, pp.326–7.

Apart from the problems of increasing membership, of defending the performing right against the music users, and of licensing, one other feature of the Society's policy between the wars stands out. This was the frequent resort to litigation. Between 1914 and 1939 the Society found itself embroiled in no fewer than thirty-five legal actions, with 1922 standing as the peak year with six cases. Resort to the Courts, frequent as it was, still represented the tiny tip of a large negotiating iceberg. In the early days litigation was mainly used to show that the rights the Society protected were legally enforceable against an unlicensed user, who could not be allowed to enjoy a more privileged position than his licensed competitor in business. By the end of the 1920s this defensive action against intransigent music users was, on the whole, no longer necessary and in the 1930s the number of such cases fell sharply. Such cases as did occur were of a different nature, and mainly arose in an effort to secure judicial interpretation of particular aspects of the 1911 Copyright Act, for example as in the case of the PRS *v.* Hawthorns Hotel (Bournemouth) Ltd in 1933 to secure the Court's verdict that a performance in a hotel lounge is a performance in public. More sophisticated than this method of legal action was action to bring new forms of musical reproduction within the scope of the Act. The growth of rediffusion services[1] posed such a problem. Up to 1931 the licence held by the BBC from the PRS extended to the public rediffusion of works in the Society's repertoire. From 1932, however, the PRS insisted on being free to deal with the rediffusion question itself, and the BBC licence was restricted to the reception of the Society's repertoire for listeners' domestic and private use. In a test case brought against Hammond's Bradford Brewery Ltd in 1933 the Court rejected the defendant's plea that the act of making audible to hotel guests musical works broadcast by the BBC was not a performance, or that, if it was, it was not provided by the hotel proprietors.

The aims of the Society as announced at its formation in 1914 were: '. . . to exercise and enforce the rights of its members, to

1. See p.33.

restrain unauthorized use of their works, and to collect fees for permission to perform the same in public'. How far had it achieved these aims and what had it done for its members in the period 1914–39? As far as the exercise and enforcement of its members' rights were concerned, the Society had undeniably achieved its aim. Both at home and abroad, through agency agreements and the creation of national performing right societies, the members of the Society were far better protected than they had been as individuals before 1914. By 1939, most music users recognized the legitimacy of the Society's operations, and those who did not were forced to do so by litigation. Outside the Courts the Society had defended its members against attacks in Parliament as in the case of the 1930 Musical Copyright Bill. At an international level the interests of the creative professions were represented at copyright conferences through the International Confederation of Authors' and Composers' Societies (CISAC), founded in 1926, with headquarters in Paris. The Society had also adopted a broad definition of 'welfare' and in 1933 a Benevolent Fund (now called the Members' Fund) had been created to assist writer members in need. On the collection of fees the Society could also claim a successful record. In 1919 the Society had 4,400 licensees; in 1939 the figure was 41,000. Admittedly the Society's aims did not translate into any clearly defined pricing criteria and the absence of any normal business criteria with which to judge the Society's record makes it difficult to assess its efficiency in this respect.[1] At all times, however, during the twenty years the Society's income, both gross and net, had kept pace with its growing membership. Indeed, perhaps the best indication of the Society's success was this very increase in membership – from thirty-nine in 1914 to 1,861 in 1939. Within that membership it seems likely that the serious composer had gained more than the popular, relative to their respective pre-1914 positions. Before the PRS was established the composer as well as the lyricist and librettist had tended to

1. An attempt will be found in Chapter 4 to assess the long-run effect of the Society on members' income.

'sell out' their rights either for a fixed sum or for other royalties which took a long time to come in and entailed a great expense in collection. As John Ireland said in 1924:

'To a composer of popular ballads, the sale of whose "successes" runs into six figures and whose income is profitable to the super-tax col-lector, perhaps the advantage of the PRS may be negligible; but the composer of serious music is in quite a different position, and to him I consider a great service is done by this Society which helps him to live by his work.'[1]

A similar view was expressed by Charles Volkert, the prota-gonist and publisher of Wagner, in relation to the growing im-portance of that composer's performing rights, and is worth quoting at length:

... with Wagner (his) music was principally sold for the purpose of public performances, arrangements of every kind being inadequate and unsatisfactory and also difficult. Without the performing right, we were very slow in getting a return for our outlay. ... It is absolutely impossible to calculate the loss of income composers like Wagner, Verdi, Gounod, Brahms, Dvořák, Grieg or Sullivan sustained in Bri-tain for forty years by the practical confiscation of the performing right especially because most were in the habit of selling copyright out-right ...
The average of successful works by most composers is one in twenty. In lighter and short-lived works ... the average is rather better, but in songs hardly one in fifty outlives five years, or gets home at all, and still composers offer them in shoals. Serious real music takes longer to get known, but it lasts longest ... yet requires the PRS to look after it, while it gradually becomes appreciated and productive ... the per-forming right has enabled me to make investments in musical works, some of which are locked up for years, and I have done this more liberally since performing right became an institution in England.[2]

By 1939 it could truly be claimed for the Society that it had helped to create 'order out of chaos', at least in one area of the music market.

1. *The PR Gazette*, 1924.   2. *Ibid.*

The Mechanical Recording Right 1914–39

. . . no industry ought to be permitted to flourish upon the methods of the highwayman . . .[1]

The circumstances surrounding the request in 1927 by the Musical Copyright Defence Association (MCDA) to the Board of Trade for a public inquiry into the rate of royalty on records have already been discussed.[2] The result of the inquiry is well known – the royalty rate was raised 25 per cent from 5 per cent to $6\frac{1}{4}$ per cent of 'the ordinary retail selling price of the contrivance'. This in no way matched the 100 per cent increase which had been sought by the MCDA, and the royalty rate remained a source of discontent amongst composers. Less well known perhaps[3] was the information which the Inquiry uprooted about the place of the recording industry in the music market. Some of the evidence was predictable: the testimony to the fall in sheet music sales as a result of the growing popularity of records; the complaints about the decrease in the royalty per record as a result both of the cut price competition between record manufacturers and the use of 'company songs' or non-copyright material on one side of the disc. The most interesting discussion centred in the question of who was responsible for the commercial success of records and what the division of rewards should be. On this the MCDA had no doubts: 'the composer is the source and origin of the success of these mechanical reproductions'.[4] This the record companies were quite prepared to concede, for it then raised the question of why the publishers were receiving 40 per cent of the record royalty, the customary division of royalty then being 10 per cent to the publisher or a society as a fee for collection, with the balance divided 40 per cent to the composer, 30 per cent to the author, and 30 per cent to the publisher. As

1. 1928 Copyright Royalty (Mechanical Musical Instruments) Inquiry, opening submission for MCDA.
2. See pp.15–17.
3. The minutes of evidence were never published. A single manuscript copy exists in the Department of Trade and Industry.
4. 1928 Copyright Royalty (etc.), Inquiry.

Counsel for the Mechanical Music Industry submitted:

'Our case is that nearly the whole of the trouble here is caused by the unnecessary share of the mechanical royalties which pass into the hands of the music publishers – they are a close body, they make the composers assign their mechanical rights to them – the publishers take 10 per cent for commission and then 30 per cent as a share. The gramophone companies believe they will be able to get the composers to come direct to them.[1]

Here was a struggle between the recording companies and the music publishers not just for the composer's heart and mind but also his purse. Was publication still vital for the creation of a market, and was it now legitimate to say that: 'the mechanical instrument makers only reproduce works which have already become successful. They take no risks and reap the full advantage'?[2]

In fact, little evidence was produced by recording companies to substantiate their complaint that the publishers obtained an undue and inequitable share of royalties, and the Committee accepted that:

In many cases the publisher performs an important role in bringing out and popularizing a work. The manufacturers seldom if ever bring out a new work or procure its initial popularity. They often extend its popularity when once it has been initiated by a publisher or created by production on the stage or by reason of publication in another country.[3]

Despite this reaffirmation of the importance of the publisher, the picture of the music market which emerged was one of rapid change, and one in which the publishers were having to swiftly adjust their traditional activities to meet changed conditions. The music market, on the demand side, was clearly split into three categories:

1 Classical (both old and new) and Educational;
2 the Ballad and Victorian; and
3 the Jazz dance or American type.

1. *Ibid.*, Opening statement for Mechanical Music Industry.
2. *Ibid.*, Minutes of Evidence.   3. *Ibid.*, Report, p.9.

In each of these three markets the costs and risks of publishers and recording companies were different.

In the third category some 90 per cent of the music used in records was reputed to be American in origin. The British manufacturer was simply exploiting works which were already well established in the States. Whilst this lessened initial costs and risks, the high and rapid rate of obsolescence in this section – Alfred Clarke, Managing Director of the Gramophone Company claimed that 85 per cent of his productions lasted only a year or less, and between 9 per cent and 24 per cent were absolutely useless after the same period – made for a high turnover. The 'American invasion' also meant that the British publisher who had traditionally survived on the royalty ballad was having to forge new links with American publishing firms to secure permission to exploit the original copyright. However, with the establishment of matrix exchanges between us and British recording companies, the publishers' grip on the market was being prised away. The publisher's traditional skills were to some extent irrelevant in the face of technological advance. Nor was technological advance the only factor taking business from the publisher, for new methods of retailing records, especially the cheap editions, completely by-passed the usual channels. 'Instead of going to the music publishers or music shops, they went to the drapers, the grocers and the gardeners, and pushed in through new channels, and found a new public.'

How extensive this new retailing pattern was in the inter-war period is difficult to say. Woolworth's 6d novelty records established a place for record sales in that large retail group, and the addition of record selling to the business of gramophone and wireless retailers was also widespread. The traditional music publishing firm was a business under pressure in the 1920s and 1930s. For the composer of serious music these changes faced him with new problems. Although the evidence suggested that the demand for classical and educational music showed some increase, there was no guarantee that with pressure on the music publishers the practice of subsidizing serious composition through the profits on popular music would be maintained.

According to the evidence submitted to the Inquiry by five of the English gramophone companies, nearly £200,000 had been paid by them in 1927 in mechanical royalties to copyright owners. Whilst not entirely a matter of new income to composers and authors, this sum, the Inquiry concluded, represented a far greater use of their work by the public than before the gramophone was invented. The record companies argued that composers and authors had no serious grounds for complaint if their incomes remained as large as they were before mechanical recording. The Inquiry disagreed, and thought that the increased use merited a higher rate of return. The result was the increased award of a $6\frac{1}{4}$ per cent royalty. It is perhaps worthwhile comparing the £200,000 mechanical royalty income with the income of the Performing Right Society in the same year of £116,000 to gain an idea of the relative value of the two markets. One other feature of the award may also be mentioned. The royalty rate was set for fourteen years and could not be altered by Act of Parliament. This feature had, of course, quite different implications for composers and recording companies. The latter gained price stability in their main raw material cost whilst the composer stood to gain only if record prices rose.[1] In the 1930s they fell.

There was one other major development concerning mechanical reproduction during the 1930s. This was the decision in the case of the Gramophone Company Ltd *v.* Stephen Carwardine & Co. (1933) where it was held that the 'special' copyright under Section 19 of the 1911 Copyright Act included a public performing right in the recording as such, independent of the copyright, if any, in the work recorded. The 'special' copyright when granted in 1911 was originally considered to have been solely designed to protect manufacturers against the copying of their

---

1. This statement does not entirely cover the situation. If the price of records fell and more were purchased by consumers as a result, then it might be possible for the composer's total income from record royalties to increase despite the lower sum received per record sold, *cf.* the situation when record prices rise and sales fall.

recordings by rival competitors,[1] its main aim being to prevent
the piracy of technical improvements.[2] The decision that it included an ancillary performing right belonging to the record
manufacturer led to the incorporation of Phonographic Performance Ltd in 1934 to try to control this right. Like the Performing Right Society, Phonographic Performance was a company limited by guarantee and without share capital. It was
established to deal with applications for licences to use records
as a means of public performance over the whole field of entertainment from 'cinemas right down to the Vicar's garden party'.[3]
At first, after the Carwardine case, licences were freely issued.
The fear, however, that public performances of records would
hit record sales, and pressures from the Musicians' Union, who
were alarmed at the likely effect of gramophone performances on
the employment of 'live' musicians, led to an increasingly restrictive licensing policy. Unlike the PRS, which would not refuse
a licence so long as the royalty was forthcoming, willingness to
pay did not guarantee the record user a licence from Phonographic Performance. Like the PRS, PPL developed a series of
tariffs to cover all forms of public performance, with rates varied
between different classes of performance. As far as the copyright
owner was concerned, one fundamental and very important
difference existed between the two societies. The basis of distribution of performance royalties between composer, author
and publisher was laid down in the PRS constitution. No such
fundamental guarantees existed with the PPL. By law it was
quite entitled to retain all the money it collected. However, the
first Chairman of Phonographic Performance,[4] Sir Louis Sterling, saw to it that the revenue derived from these licence fees
was distributed not merely amongst record manufacturers but

1. Copinger and Skone James, *op. cit.*, paragraph 775.
2. For a good discussion of the origin of the provision in the 1911 Act, see *Report
   of the Copyright Committee* (1952), Cmnd. 8662, paragraph 140.
3. *Report of the Copyright Committee* (1952), Cmnd. 8662, paragraph 143.
4. See article by Reynell Wreford, 'Writers and Records', in *Performing Right*,
   1965.

also as *ex gratia* payments to recording artists, performing musicians and music publishers. The basis of distribution under this voluntary system was 20 per cent of the net distributable revenue for the benefit of recording artists, 12½ per cent for the Musicians' Union, and a further 10 per cent to the music publishers. Whether or not these fees received by the publishers were passed on to the original composer or author depended on individual agreements with publishers.

Until the introduction of the 1956 Copyright Act, performing right in gramophone records remained the only ancillary right in existence. As such, it raised few problems before the Second World War. With the increased importance of access to the mass media, the impact of new methods of recording on musicians, and the demand for the establishment of other ancillary rights by film and television producers, the whole subject of ancillary rights became of great importance after 1945. These developments will be discussed in Chapter 4.

4
The Music Market
1939-70

... no one nowadays need fear the agony of complete silence ...[1]

... music 'untouched by hand': the art of a technological mind ...[2]

Introduction

By 1939 much of the unrelieved gloom surrounding the impact of 'mechanical music' on the music industry had given way to a cautious optimism about the future. It was clear by the end of the 1930s that the gramophone, the cinema and the wireless had not resulted in a total 'economic and technical pogrom'. Better organization amongst composers and professional musicians, as well as the restrictions placed on the new media by vested interests in the music industry, had tempered the impact of mechanical music. The triumph of the new media over the traditional forms of musical activity was less than complete not just because of these restrictions but also because the new media still had considerable technical deficiencies so far as musical reproduction was concerned. Despite electrical recording, the gramophone was still 'an expensive and troublesome hobby'[3] and its impact had been felt mainly at the popular end of the music market. The number of public concerts too did not appear to have diminished despite the wireless for 'many people take

1. E. D. Mackerness, *op. cit.*, p.273.
2. A. Milner, 'Music and the Radio', in *Twentieth Century Music*, ed. R. H. Myers, London, 1968.
3. R. W. Wood, 'The Future of Music Making', *Musical Times*, February 1939, p.95.

delight in *seeing* musical performers as well as in hearing them'.[1] With serious music, wireless reception was still held to be less than adequate except on expensive receivers.[2] By 1939 it was clear that wireless, whatever effect it had in altering the tastes of the pre-radio music public, had created a new public all of its own. Although no music critic in the 1930s was ever quite clear what the economic and social characteristics of this new audience were, it was evident that 'the great unmusical class' would be a factor of considerable importance in the subsequent shaping of the music market.

One difficulty in attempting to discuss the market for musical composition has been the lack of any adequate measure of the extent of the market. From the side of demand a market is usually described in terms not merely of the number of consumers but also of their total expenditure on the product, and it has only been possible to indicate indirectly the size of some individual components of the market, e.g. through the growth in the number of wireless licences or in the number of cinema visits. Another approach to measuring the growth in demand for musical composition, and one which may help to place the period between 1939 and 1970 in some kind of perspective, can be had from the licensing activities of the Performing Right Society. In 1924 the Society issued 5,487 licences for the public performance of music. Calculations by the New Business Department of the Society in the early 1930s suggested that the saturation point for the Society's licensing business in the UK lay between 48,000 and 50,000 licences. With 41,000 licences issued in 1938 the Society seemed well set to achieve this goal.

1. *Ibid.*
2. E. D. Mackerness, *op. cit.*, p.268.
   The gramophone was always ahead of wireless in the quality of sound reproduction. This was because broadcasting on overcrowded Medium and Long Wavebands was subject to a 9,000-cycle bandwidth limitation: i.e. the broadcast carrier wave could not accommodate sound frequencies above 9 k/cs. The great breakthrough into broadcast high fidelity came in the 1950s with the introduction of frequency modulation with a more or less unlimited bandwidth. This technical reason probably retarded the growth in the audience for serious music.

Although a large part of this impressive increase must have been due simply to better 'policing' and the greater acceptance by music users of the performing right, the rise in the number of licences may also be taken as indicative of the growth in the demand for musical composition. Whilst these figures alone cast doubt on the more gloomy prognoses of the mechanical music 'disease' of the inter-war years, the rise in licence figures since 1939 has been even more spectacular. By the mid-1960s the growth in the demand for music for public performance brought the number of licences to the 100,000 mark.[1] The last period of this study has seen a remarkable expansion in the market for musical composition, and it is the aim of this chapter to examine this growth and describe the nature of the composer's market at present.

The Second World War 1939–45

Whatever the unspecified nature of the chrysalid 'great un-musical public' whose demand for music was emerging prior to 1939, there is little doubt that the origins of the post-1945 growth in demand stretch back to the war years. As in 1914 the immediate effects of the Second World War were extremely disruptive to musical activity. Early government restrictions on the evening opening hours of theatres and concert halls resulted in a loss of income and employment to composers and musicians.[2] The initial confinement of broadcasting to one wavelength and the cessation of the infant television service further limited composers' outlets. With the exception of the period of heavy air raids during the summer of 1940,[3] the disruption of public entertainment proved remarkably short lived and with entertainment one of the few goods 'off-ration' the high public demand for relaxation and entertainment brought boom conditions to the

---

1. E. Ford, 'The Composer's Expanding Market', *Performing Right*, October 1965.
2. Letter in the *Musical Times* from Leslie Boosey, November 1939, p.771.
3. E. D. Mackerness, *op. cit.*, p.266.

leisure industries. Dance halls, night clubs and theatres benefited, whilst in the cinema 'average weekly attendances increased from nineteen million in 1945, and gross box-office receipts were nearly trebled'.[1] With wireless the position was
slightly different. Although 'the habit of listening became more
widespread in Britain than ever before'[2] scarcity of wireless
components and sets actually resulted in a fall in the number of
licences in 1940 and 1941.[3] Thereafter the number of radio
licences, which had stood at 8·9 million in 1938, increased to
10·8 million by 1946. These figures by themselves do not however indicate the full extent of the increased demand for music in
this particular section of the music market, for it was in radio,
more than anywhere else, that the demand of the 'great un-
musical public' was expressed. Since its foundation, the B B C had
always catered for music in leisure situations, but what was novel
in 1940 was the new demand for music in work situations.
'Music while you work' started in June 1940, and was specially
designed to be suitable for rediffusion in factories.[4] In the same
way that the Forces Programme was designed to increase
morale and provide entertainment for the Armed Services,
'Music while you work' was intended to boost and sustain the
efforts of the civilian labour force. Background music, it was
held, took the boredom and fatigue out of repetitive and routine
work. Certainly its popularity was marked, and by 1944 8,000
factories employing over $4\frac{1}{2}$ million people were said to be
listening to the programme. If this development did not quite
amount to the 'audible wallpaper' description of radio music in
the 1960s, it may still trace its origins to these wartime developments. Nor was music in factories the only new market to
open up for, by the end of the war, music was to be heard in 'air-
raid shelters, rest centres . . . factory canteens, workers hostels,

1. P E P *The British Film Industry*, London, 1952.
2. A. Briggs, *op. cit.*, Vol.I I I, p.69.
3. This divergence between licence figures, on which the composer's remuneration
   was based through the broadcasting right, and the true audience for his music
   was to be significant when the 'transistor explosion' occurred.
4. C. F. James, *op. cit.*, p.97.

village halls and public parks and in camps and on remote battery sites'.[1]

The content of the B B C's music programmes during the war is of some interest. In table 4.1 the breakdown of the music content of the B B C's output between 1939 and 1944 is given. As can be seen, light music dominated in the Forces Programme, whilst in the Home Service classical music and light music enjoyed a rough parity of broadcasting time. These figures however camouflage the fierce debate which raged over the quality of the B B C's light music and dance music output. Debates over the quality of the B B C's music output were, as we have seen in Chapter 3, nothing new, but in 1942 an attempt was made to eliminate 'crooning, sentimental numbers, drivelling words, slush, innuendos and so on'.[2] The new policy was attacked by the Music Publishers' Association as dictatorial and as not justified by any change in public demand. Again, the old problem was the B B C's lack of any means of determining exactly what the public wanted, and although listener research was meant to be 'the equivalent of a non-commercial box-office' there was always the feeling within the B B C that programme content should not be heavily influenced by listener research. Whilst this tended to mean a greater share in programme output for the serious composer, the attempt to alter the quality of light music and dance music programmes faced popular and light composers and publishers with the problem of trying to seek some guidance on what was acceptable to the B B C. Until 1947 the popular song-writers had no organized means of placing their views before the B B C except individually or through their publishers. This assumed a harmony of interest which was not always evident, and with the formation of the Songwriters' Guild in 1947 new methods of protecting the popular composers' interests were evolved.

The serious composer had fewer grounds for complaint about

---

1. See C. F. James, *op. cit.*, p.103 quoting a message from R. A. Butler (now Lord Butler) to P R S Annual Luncheon in 1944.
2. A. Briggs, *op. cit.*, Vol.I I I, p.578.

Table 4.1 Programme Constituents: One week in October, 1939–44 inclusive percentage of total transmission time

	1939	1940		1941		1942		1943		1944	
		Forces	Home	Forces	Home	Forces	Home	Forces	Home	Forces	Home
Classical music	15·97	2·54	17·80	1·28	13·41	6·00	12·27	4·75	15·88	5·31	9·62
Light music	26·15	31·57	16·21	30·12	16·52	27·02	13·53	30·88	12·14	23·10	13·66
Dance music	5·10	11·97	6·39	12·43	6·47	12·27	4·00	14·08	7·30	8·93	8·68
Gramophone records	4·22	18·34	5·08	16·47	6·05	17·69	8·88	17·94	9·23	19·08	11·72
Light entertainment	7·04	15·70	6·38	19·65	4·75	15·01	4·55	12·08	4·37	17·07	6·82
Total time (hours and minutes)	120·45	98·10	121·20	116·10	121·20	115·30	121·20	115·30	121·20	115·30	121·20

Source: A. Briggs, op. cit., Vol.III, pp.596–7.

the BBC's wartime music policy. Serious music gained a wider and more knowledgeable audience during the war. As table 4.1 shows, within the increased hours of broadcasting classical music received a considerable increase in time. This increase also extended to the broadcasting of serious music from gramophone records and between 1942 and 1944 this rose from 6 per cent of gramophone record output to 40 per cent.[1] For the British composer what was important was not just the amount of time devoted to serious music as such but the place accorded to the works of British composers within the total. Despite a policy of encouraging new composition and British works, less than a third of the time devoted to serious music was supplied from British composers. Like the popular songwriters, the serious composers formed themselves into a Guild partly with the aim of securing better representation on radio. This was a task which was made easier with the introduction of the BBC's Third Programme in 1946 specifically designed to cater for minority 'highbrow' tastes.

Two wartime bodies which helped to satisfy 'the apparently unquenchable thirst for music'[2] were the Entertainments National Service Association (ENSA), and the Council for the Encouragement of Music and the Arts (CEMA). Although the immediate importance of these bodies lay in providing wartime entertainment for both troops and civilians, the longer-term significance for music of CEMA was that it ultimately involved an explicit recognition that the government had a role to play in fostering the arts, and the reconstitution of CEMA into the Arts Council in 1946 maintained this policy. Public sponsorship through the Arts Council was given to ballet, opera, orchestras and festivals and, as far as serious music was concerned, helped to ease the more restrictive effects of commercial pressures in matters like programme content. Public patronage for serious music was not limited to the BBC and the Arts Council. The British Council was given the task of 'exporting' British culture abroad at the taxpayer's expense, and some contemporary com-

1. A. Briggs, *op. cit.*, p.583.   2. E. D. Mackerness, *op. cit.*, p.268.

posers benefited from this.[1] Post-war subsidies provide a good instance of support for the media resulting in an increased supply of musical composition. With the Royal Opera House, Covent Garden, now subsidized out of public funds as a 'National' Opera, and Sadler's Wells as a secondary one, London had two theatres devoted to opera and ballet. The openings these offered to composers resulted in an increase in ballet composition.[2]

Post-1945

Despite the apparent popularity of serious music during the war, by 1945 doubts were being expressed about its future in the post war world. As with the period after 1918, it seemed unlikely that when consumer goods became freely available on the market musical activity would attract as many supporters as during the war, 'the new audience for serious music (being) drawn away by other pursuits once more available in peacetime'.[3] The financial troubles of opera and of the large provincial symphony orchestras seemed to be supporting evidence for these fears. On the other hand, their difficulties can be ascribed to the changed nature of the public's demand for music. Opera in Britain had always been an extremely risky business proposition in view of the relatively restricted audience for this form of music drama. As for orchestras, the high costs involved in maintaining permanent orchestras, partly increased by the high rates for players set by the Musicians' Union, together with the existence of alternative media in the radio and gramophone, militated against the success of the public concert.

The Technology of Musical Reproduction

For the listener, however, the post-war world held out many benefits. In 1948 the American Columbia Recording Company issued the first long-playing discs at $33\frac{1}{3}$ r.p.m. Unlike earlier

1. H. Pelling, *Modern Britain 1885–1955*, London, 1960, p.194.
2. D. Hussey, 'A Survey of Contemporary Music in the United Kingdom' in R. H. Myers (Ed.), *op. cit.*, pp.215–23.   3. The PRS Bulletin, August 1945, p.96.

technological innovations in records, 'the long-playing record as
a commercial proposition was the practical fulfilment of a long
expectation rather than a novelty'.[1] The LP both increased the
quantity of music available to the listener: 'you can go away for
a weekend with several operas, symphonies, string quartets and
odd bits and pieces in your suitcase and hardly notice the extra
weight!'[2] and allowed him to select from the best performances
of a very few top-quality musicians. If the advent of the long-
playing record 'was an answer to prayer'[2] the subsequent confusion arising from the issue of the 45 r.p.m. record by the Victor
Record Company in 1948, and the obsolescence of record players
were less welcome features of these innovations for music consumers. By the early 1950s the manufacture of record players
with twin pick-up heads and three-speed gears solved the problem of the variety of discs now available. The long-playing record brought with it an extension in the recorded repertoire
beyond all predictions. With the extended-play record it helped
to boost record sales during the 1950s. Meanwhile further research was being carried out into sound frequencies, and in 1958
the stereo record became a commercial reality.

Although attempts to increase the playing time of records
dated back to before the First World War,[3] the interval between the start of the CBS research team's work in 1944 and the
commercial exploitation of the LP record four years later was
remarkably short. This was not the case with the magnetic tape
recorder. Although invented in 1899 by Valdemar Poulsen, it
had to wait the development of electronic amplifiers to make
it a viable commercial proposition. Retail sales of reel-to-reel
recorded tapes began in 1956.[4] Despite this time lag, the tape
recorder radically influenced recording technology and the
structure of the record industry.

Before 1939 the record market in Britain was dominated by

1. A. Robertson, 'A New Age in Recorded Music', *Musical Times*, May 1953.
2. *Ibid.*
3. Neophone (England) tried in 1904 and RCA (America) in 1931.
4. L. G. Wood, 'The Growth and Development of the Recording Industry', *The Gramophone*, 1971, p.801.

three large manufacturers. By 1970 the market was shared by eight large manufacturers and between fifty and sixty smaller ones. The appearance of these new firms owed much to the tape recorder. Before the introduction of magnetic tape recording, recording took place on a wax disc from which all subsequent copies were made. Any errors were either permanently inscribed on the master disc or else the master had to be re-taken, an expensive and time-consuming business. With magnetic tape it became feasible to record during a number of sessions, each of short duration. This ensured a high degree of perfection and the final master tape came about as an edited version of the best of 'the takes'. Multitrack recording allowed tracks to be combined in a variety of ways so as to achieve sound effects quite different from the original performance. The gap between a 'live' performance and a performance on record became wider than ever before and the elimination of faulty bars and chords from a recorded performance meant that 'many recordings are mosaics to a greater or lesser degree'.[1] By cutting down the high capital requirements needed to begin record production, the tape recorder lowered the costs of entry to the industry. One result of this was the creation of numerous small independent record companies. These took over some of the functions of older established enterprises. They discovered and contracted artists themselves, developed the recording to master tape stage and then licensed it, against a royalty payment to an established record company. The older established record companies were not the only section of the music industry to be influenced by this development. One of the major functions of music publishers before the tape recorder appeared was to seek out recording contracts for composers and artists. This function was short-circuited by the independent record producers.[2] One reaction by

1. A. Milner, 'Music and the Radio' in *Twentieth Century Music*, ed. R. H. Myers, London, 1968.
2. It has been suggested to us that the movement into independent record production was spurred on by the unwillingness of music publishers to exploit new popular music by British composers at a time when public preference strongly favoured American pop music.

music publishers to this development was their movement into recording for themselves and selling records under their own label. Another response to this competition came with the creation of a teenage record market in the late 1950s.[1] Large numbers of small pop groups began to write and record their own material, forming small record companies to do so. Music publishers were able to create a new demand for their skills by providing management services for these small companies.

Other stages of record production also experienced substantial change. Plastic was first used to replace shellac, a breakable and expensive material, in LP records. The development of special plastics enabled record production to be more highly automated both at the moulding and pressing stages of production.[2]

Although reel-to-reel recorded tapes were suitable for private performance, they suffered from the disadvantage of having to be threaded on to reproducing equipment. This limited their usefulness for public performances. In 1965 the threading problem was overcome when the cartridge form of recorded tape was introduced. The cassette was a later parallel development and both innovations opened up new markets for recorded material in supplying 'background' music in pubs, theatres, bingo halls, railway stations, airport lounges and restaurants. Like the LP record, the result of these innovations was to create additional markets for music rather than to simply replace existing methods of musical reproduction.

Electronic Music

Musical composition was also radically altered by developments in electronics. Over little more than the last quarter of a century electronics have created a new branch of musical composition. Electronic music and concrete music are based on a fairly simple

1. For this development see pp.109–10.
2. See L. G. Wood, *op. cit.*, for a full discussion of new recording processes. This section leans heavily on his excellent article.

principle. It is to record any sounds, musical or natural, on magnetic tape and then put them through various processes before combining them to form a piece of 'electronic' or 'concrete' music.[1] The sounds could be distorted by being put through various filters to remove different frequencies from them or played backwards or at any speed or pitch, thus giving rise to an enormous number of possible combinations. Electronic music drew on the theory of physics as much as on the theory of music and demanded a new range of skills. One result of this has been that its main practitioners were technicians rather than professional composers.[2] Composers working in this field needed 'knowledge of mathematics, tape or film editing, computers, acoustics, sound recording and of course, music'.[3] Even within the short span of its existence the techniques involved have undergone substantial modification. The earliest method of composition involved the composer not only in planning his music, but also in the method of carrying it out:

'This process consists of recording sounds and subsequently modifying them both physically (by cutting, etc.) and electronically (by filtering etc.). The piece is slowly assembled and its component parts are copied and mixed on to second and third 'generation' recordings. Eventually the whole composition is joined up and completed, and a final copy is made embodying . . . everything he thought of at the beginning.'[4]

The slowness and risk of mistakes in this 'classical' method led to the development of a more automated technique:

'In this process the score is translated into a symbolic language which is fed into the store of a computer. The machine then . . . directly operates the equipment producing the sound, carrying out all the instructions on the score, so that processes which were previously done at the second or third generation stage are now performed before anything has been recorded. Depending upon the complexity of the music,

1. H. Searle, 'Experimental Media: 1' in R. H. Myers (ed.), *op. cit.*, pp.140–6.
2. *Ibid.*
3. R. E. Dolan, *Music in Modern Media*, New York, 1967, pp.164–73.
4. T. Cary 'Electronic Music Today', in *Musical Times*, 1968, pp. 31–2.

it should be possible to programme the machine to "play" the music in its final form, and it is then only necessary to record it once.'[1]

Although the electronic composer has not abdicated and given his creative responsibilities to the machine, electronic music is 'the apotheosis of mechanical reproduction in music: the sounds are synthetic and the instrument that produces them is the amplifier. Thus we have music "untouched by hand": the art of a technological mind'.[2]

Radio – Television

Improvements in recording were matched by developments in radio and television. The BBC's television service was re-introduced in 1947 and under a five year plan announced in November 1949 a nation-wide service was created. Contemporary opinion on the likely impact of the service varied widely. Leslie Boosey, then Chairman of the PRS, asked 'is it going to supersede sound broadcasting?' and answered 'I doubt it myself . . . it is much more costly than sound broadcasting. You can't turn it on and leave it to its own devices'.[3] This, in the short run at least was a fairly accurate forecast. Television receivers were expensive, programme hours were limited, and television did seem to demand undivided attention. As can be seen from table 4.2, the number of television licences grew very slowly in the first five years and much more slowly than radio had in the 1920s (see table 3.1, p. 64). Whilst the BBC was criticized for being dominated by 'sound radio consciousness' this could be justified by

1. *Ibid.*
2. A. Milner, *op. cit.*
   These developments in the techniques of sound-production have presented the performance right societies with delicate problems, the resolution of which is not yet clear. These concern the acceptability for membership of engineers who undoubtedly contribute to the production of the electronic work but have none of the traditional musical skills, and the valuation (of which duration is traditionally the basic element) of the electronic work for distribution purposes. Similar problems are obviously posed by aleatoric music.
3. At the PRS Annual Luncheon for Members 1948.

the relative size of the audiences for radio and television. Still, as the number of viewers grew, the price of sets began to fall and by 1956–7 there were as many people watching television as listening to wireless. Moreover with the introduction of commercial television, following the Independent Television Act of 1955,[1] there was a wider range of programme choice and licence figures rose markedly. The impact of television on the older

Table 4.2   *Numbers of Sound and Television Licences*

	Number of Sound only (at £1)	Number of Sound and Television (at £2)
1947	10,712,970	7,467
1948	10,970,085	32,994
1949	11,314,450	92,784
1950	11,875,368	239,345
1951	11,626,498	586,601

forms of entertainment varied. Cinema was worst hit and exhibitors began to bemoan 'the missing millions'. Competition from television was especially severe because unlike in the 1930s, when both radio and cinema enjoyed expanding markets, cinema audiences had already begun to fall from their almost freak post-war heights when television became popular.[2] Due to the relatively slow growth of its audience the initial effect of television on entertainments such as theatre and sport was limited. This was not the only reason. Commercial interests from the entertainment world took measures to safeguard their interest. For example, the Association for the Protection of Copyright in Sport banned all television at sporting events organized by its members. Theatre, music hall and concert hall proprietors operated similar restrictions for a time as well.[3]

Although television became 'the most congenial form of mass communication' its effect on musical culture appears to have

1. For discussion of the loss of the BBC monopoly, see p.108.
2. PEP, *op. cit.*, p.290.
3. For a discussion of these and other restrictions, see p.116ff.

been surprisingly limited.[1] It created a new demand for background music and 'theme tunes' from popular programmes became a not infrequent feature of the all important hit parade.[2] As far as serious music was concerned it did not, any more than radio had done, supplant the concert hall as the prime medium. The purely visual element of television has not been critical for the appreciation of serious music. Even ballet and opera, the most likely benefactors from television, have not come over well onto the small screen, because they become 'oddly miniaturized if presented in the normal way.'[3] The expense of mounting full-scale productions, the minority audience and the interrupted nature of family viewing have also detracted from the possibilities of television as a means of presenting these types of musical performance. Technical difficulties limited television's impact on the demand for serious music. Three particular problems prevented good sound quality: producers had to compromise between sound quality and the intrusion of boom microphones; the transmission of television sound on an adjacent frequency to vision raised the old bandwidth problem, and television sets could accommodate only small speakers with insufficient 'baffling'. Transistors have alleviated some of these problems. Their use has increased the size of loudspeakers and the space available for them (thereby increasing the quality of bass reproduction), and the switch to UHF transmission has increased the range of transmitted frequencies (thereby improving the reproduction of treble and harmonic frequencies).

If television as such did not directly influence musical culture, the institutional framework under which it expanded did. With the loss of its television monopoly in 1955 the BBC found itself faced with competition from ITV. Wherever BBC and commercial programmes were in competition it was soon apparent that the latter were generally more popular. By 1960 a clear picture had emerged of between 60 per cent and 70 per cent of viewing time

1. E. D. Mackerness, *op. cit.*, p.280.
2. For changes in the pop music market, see p.101–25.
3. E. D. Mackerness, *op. cit.*, p.282.

going to commercial broadcasting and between 30 and 40 per cent to the BBC.[1] With the concurrent increase in the television audience the BBC in 1957 in an effort to save money to fight the competition from ITV announced a series of 'adjustments' to the existing pattern of sound broadcasting.[2] These included a cut in the Third Programme by 45 per cent to three hours nightly and the introduction of a new Network Three to cater mainly for 'popular' minority interests. For serious composers these cuts were exceedingly critical. As one of the two main channels for serious music, especially symphonic and chamber music, outside performances, publishing and recording opportunities were all highly dependent on access to the Third Programme. Although some partial restoration was undertaken in the following year when two hours of broadcasting – on Saturdays only – were added to the Third Programme, the cuts seemed to minority interests only too clearly to amount to 'a retreat on all fronts in the face of the advance of competitive television'.[3]

The programme changes of 1957 had another unintended result. The new Network Three, designed to cater for 'popular' minority interests, was to take over a large part of the pop music content of the Light Programme. Instead of gaining 'The Younger Generation Audience' as planned,[4] the BBC actually lost over a million teenage listeners.[5] At a time when 'the kingdom of teenagers was at hand'[6] this left a large potential audience with a frustrated demand for pop music. Moreover, the programme changes also misinterpreted the effect of television on radio. Despite the fact that the television audience was larger than the radio audience, 'steam radio' was by no means dead and

1. A. Marwick, *Britain in the Century of Total War*, London, 1968, p.438.
2. *Report of the (Pilkington) Committee on Broadcasting*, 1960, Vol.II, App. E. Cmnd. 1819–1, Paper No. 267, p.1246.
3. *Ibid.*, p.1247.
4. For discussion of the teenage audience see below.
5. Report (etc.) 1960, p.1247.
6. C. Booker, *The Neophiliacs*, London, 1969, p.235. Page references are to the Fontana edition, published 1970.

buried. With the development of transistor sets it was on the verge of staging a remarkably healthy comeback. This revival did not however benefit the BBC for two reasons. The first was that the vacuum created by the unsatisfactory state of the BBC's popular music programmes was filled, not by the BBC, but by the pop 'pirates'. Taking advantage of the BBC's conservative pop music policy (which was partly due to the BBC's sound monopoly and partly to the Musicians' Union restriction on the broadcasting of pop records) offshore radio stations began day-long unauthorized broadcasting of pop records. It was a measure of the unsatisfied demand for pop music that the first of the radio pirates could claim – according to a Gallup Poll – an audience of around seven million regular listeners.[1] The second reason was that the growth in the radio audience was not matched by any increase in the revenue from radio licences as wholesale evasion was taking place.

These features of broadcasting in the 1960s were also un-satisfactory to the composer. Although three pirate organiza-tions did make some small payments to the PRS for copyright material, they were still infringing copyright as the material was being used without permission. Likewise, even though the BBC recaptured its pop music audience after the pirates were – albeit belatedly – driven from the seas by legislation in 1966 [2] and after the BBC's pop programmes were remodelled, evasion of licence fees meant that the true audience for the composer's work was persistently understated. Broadcasting royalties suf-fered accordingly.

The farce of the pirate radio stations, for such it really was, sits oddly alongside the last of the technological improvements which have influenced communications since 1945: the space satellite. In 1900 the size of the composer's audience was vir-tually restricted by the physical capacity of the concert hall or the music hall. The gramophone and the cinema, both invented before the First World War but not fully exploited

1. C. Booker, *ibid.*, p.236.
2. By the Marine and Broadcasting (Offences) Act.

until after 1918, increased the demand for musical composition but left the fragmented nature of the audience unchanged. Radio was the first of the media to break down the barriers to mass communication. Television added the visual image but both were limited by the power of their transmitters. The communications satellite first launched in 1966 as a direct development from the 'Sputnik' of 1957 now makes it possible for a performance to reach a global audience.

However beneficial these innovations were for the listener, the problem for the composer remained the old one of ensuring that his work would be heard. With the establishment of the Composers' Guild and the Songwriters' Guild, serious and popular composers now had organizations which could take up issues such as the amount of 'British Music on British Air'. The attempts by the Guilds to further the interests of their members generally ran along two lines. The first and more negative aspect of their work involved attempts to place restrictions on the amount of foreign music used in this country. The second and more positive approach was to attempt to popularize or advertise the work of British composers and thereby increase the demand for their services.

The 'import-replacement' policy, which was what the former approach involved, ultimately resolved into attempts to exert influence on the content of the BBC's music programmes. The serious composers were first off the mark in this campaign. In 1946 the Composer's Guild demanded better representation on the BBC and also requested the corporation to supply information on the number of British works being broadcast. The following year their Guild inaugurated an analysis of BBC broadcasts to check the British content of music programmes. The BBC was not alone in finding itself the object of the Guild's attentions. The new Arts Council was also approached in an effort to persuade it to give more positive help to British composers by insisting that any grant it made to a concert organization would be conditional on the performance of a proportion of British music. No success followed this move as the Arts Council refused to attach any conditions to its financial support.[1] What has been called 'Public-Body-badgering'[2] extended to trying to influence the control of work permits issued by the Ministry of Labour to foreign composers. The aim here was to make the granting of a work permit dependent on the existence of a reciprocal engagement for a British composer.[3]

The more positive side of the Composers' Guild's work included analysing the programmes of leading orchestras to reveal the percentage of works drawn from living British composers and then congratulating the musical directors and conductors with the best records. Persistent attempts were also made to persuade conductors and concert artists to play British music when touring abroad. To what extent these policies increased the demand for the works of British composers during the 1950s and 1960s cannot be ascertained and a discussion on the impact of the Guild between 1944 and 1965 concluded that 'there is far less British music being performed today by the BBC or in the concert hall than in the early days of the Guild'.[4] To some extent the differing interests within the Guild prevented its playing a more significant part. It chose, for example, to refrain from adopting a policy of selectivity when requests were made for the Guild to suggest specific items of British music for inclusion in concert programmes. Choosing amongst the works of individual members and furthering the interests of the few would have been an invidious task and would have placed too onerous a burden on the Guild form of organization.

The approach of the Songwriters' Guild to furthering its members' interests was broadly similar to that of the Composers' Guild except that, if anything, the post-war situation of British pop and light music was even more bleak. The problem for the pop composer was the dominance of American music in the British pop market. 'Import-replacement' was much less easy

1. See 'Twenty-one years of the Composers' Guild', in *Composer*, No. 16, July 1965.
2. See G. Warrack, 'The Guild in the Fifties', in *Composer*, No. 16, July 1965.
3. See 'Twenty-one years of the Composers' Guild', *loc. cit.*
4. W. Alwyn, '1066 and All that', in *Composer*, No. 16, July 1965, p.23.

to achieve because of the long-standing origins of this American dominance. It was noted above[1] how American films had proved a good 'shop-window' for American music during the 1930s. The popularity of American films remained high throughout the war and after 1945, despite the impact quota which was put on American films to save foreign exchange.[2] Peacetime Hollywood and the American recording industry were financially strong and able to back American 'super-musicals' in Britain which expanded opportunities for American songwriters. Other reasons have been suggested for the failure of a popular British musical idiom to assert itself after the war. These include the wartime raw material restrictions which hampered the British recording industry, the continuing financial troubles of the British film industry, and the wartime absence of British songwriters and artists in the Forces or entertaining troops 'live' overseas.

Of these reasons, the first may well be judged as the most important because of the changed nature of the peacetime music market. The two dominant media were now the wireless and records. To composers it seemed that success in the latter was highly related to access to the former. The feeling was that 'music *not* broadcast by the BBC can virtually find no outlet',[3] and the main complaint of the newly formed Songwriters' Guild was that the strength of American music was a direct result of plugging by the BBC.[4] The large amount of American music being broadcast in the latter half of the 1940s had a rather straightforward explanation. Because of the manpower shortages during the war, the Musicians' Union had relaxed its 'needle-time' restrictions on the use of records by the BBC. The British recording industry had however been unable to supply sufficient material because of the restrictions under which it operated.

1. See Chapter 3.
2. P. Forster, 'J. Arthur Rank and the Shrinking Screen', in M. Sissons and P. French (eds.), *The Age of Austerity 1945–51*, London, 1963, p.295.
3. *Report of the Broadcasting Committee 1949*, Appendix H, Cmnd. 8117, Paper 98, p.512.
4. The Songwriters' Guild of Great Britain, *Success Story*, pp.11–13.

This meant that the B B C drew much of its recorded material from American sources. Its popularity with listeners, including the large contingent of American service personnel stationed in the United Kingdom, assured it a prominent place in programmes. The trouble for the British composer was that American dominance, once established, became exceptionally difficult to overthrow. With the interdependence of the two media, a sort of vicious circle came into existence. So long as American music was popular, the B B C devoted a large proportion of its programmes to American music, and in 1947, at the first meeting of the British Songwriters' Protective Association, the forerunner of the Songwriters' Guild, it was reported that 'only 19 per cent of music broadcast by the B B C is British'.[1] British recording companies, dependent on investing in the most popular current style for their commercial success, reacted in turn by shying away from British music. Music publishers followed suit, and the barriers to breaking into the pop market seemed unenviably high to the British popular songwriters. One related aspect of the success of American music was the intense competition amongst British recording companies for the output of American songwriters. This took the form of bulk purchases of catalogues and exclusive licensing agreements. Another was the establishment of substantial American interests in the London music publishing business during the 1950s such that by 1959 the Songwriters' Guild claimed that 'eighty-four London music publishing companies were controlled as to 50 per cent *or more* by foreign (almost entirely American) interests'.[2]

Access to the air and recording contracts were what the British popular songwriters wanted and the ways in which attempts were made to achieve these two aims cast interesting light on the peculiar structure of the music market in the period 1945–60. Like the Composers' Guild, the Songwriters' Guild attempted to increase the demand for the services of its mem-

1. *Ibid.*, p.12.
2. *Report of the Committee on Broadcasting 1970*, Cmnd. 1819, Vol.II, Appendix E, Paper No. 135.

bers by promotional campaigns. One initial effort with some success was a 'British Music Week'.[1] Another, and much more successful effort in the long run, was the Ivor Novello Awards instituted in 1956. By highlighting the best works in the whole range of British popular music from concert ballads and novelty songs to jazz compositions and Radio and TV scores, the Awards acted as an important 'shop-window' for British pop and light music. Representations were also made by the Guild to the major recording companies in an attempt to persuade them to devote a larger proportion of their output to the works of British composers.[2] Ultimately, however, all such activities ran up against the problem that broadcasting was crucially important to the success of a composition. Exposure through the radio was thought to be the most effective way to popularize a composition. Exercising influence on the BBC was no easy task. Still enjoying its sound broadcasting monopoly and with the additional monopoly control over the fledgling television service, the BBC was decidedly unenthusiastic about any attempt to upsurp its sole right to determine programme content. From the BBC's point of view it is not hard to see why the principle of what might be called 'producer sovereignty'[3] should have been worth fighting for. When the Beveridge Committee[4] investigated broadcasting in 1949 no fewer than seventy-five interested parties, ranging from the Scottish Women's Rural Institutes Council to the National Anti-Vaccination League, sought to establish some control over programme content. Merely to concede the right of representation in choice of programme material, never mind a veto, to even one group from such a range of heterogeneous interest would indeed have been to destroy the BBC's responsibility for broadcasting. Yet, it was at least arguable that few of these interested parties were so heavily dependent for their livelihood on the BBC as were composers. A major source of the performance royalties which had been so important in alleviating the worst effects of

1. The Songwriters' Guild of Great Britain, *op. cit.*, p.14.
2. *Report of the Committee on Broadcasting, 1949, op. cit.*, Appendix H, p.512.
3. As distinct from consumer sovereignty.
4. *Report of the Committee on Broadcasting, 1949.*

'mechanical music' lay in broadcasting. Also, given the inter-dependence of the recording and broadcasting media, the com-poser's income from record royalties tended to be closely related to the frequency with which his compositions were broadcast. Moreover, other groups within the music industry were able to influence the BBC's music programmes.

As was discussed in Chapter 3, the changing technology of musical reproduction resulted in the creation of pressure groups to protect long-standing commercial interests. In some cases attempts by these groups to protect members' interests had resulted in clashes with other sections of the music industry. In the post-war music market nowhere was the clash of interest between composer, publisher and executant more acute than in broadcasting. In a memorandum to the Beveridge Committee[1] the BBC summarized the main 'restrictive practices' which constrained its activities. Of the nine restrictive practices listed, seven involved music. All but one of the seven arose from the activities of the Musicians' Union, either alone or in concert with other artists' unions. The main restrictive practice which clashed with the interests of composers was that of 'needle-time'. The Musicians' Union, through its agreement with Phonographic Performance Limited, was able to restrict the number of hours of record broadcasting. Despite the willingness of Phonographic Per-formance to allow the BBC to increase the amount of 'needle-time', the Musicians' Union refused to agree, and indeed was pressing for a further reduction. With the importance of records to the composer this restriction damaged his interests. Tele-vision as well as radio was subject to further restrictions. These included limitations on the use of programme recordings for re-peat performances, relay performances from music halls and theatres, and simultaneous television and sound broadcasts. Be-sides the Musicians' Union, two other groups were able to influence the BBC's control of programmes: show business entre-preneurs and music publishers. Some music hall and theatre managements refused to allow artists under contract to them to

1. *Ibid.*, App. H, Paper 20, p.191.

appear in television studio performances. More directly serious from the composer's point of view were the effects of an anti-plugging agreement reached between the BBC and the Music Publishers' Association covering the exploitation of popular music. This agreement, which the BBC concluded without consulting composers,[1] limited the amount of money that might be paid to singers or orchestra leaders to meet the cost of the special orchestrations needed to adapt a piece of music to the style or instruments of the performer. By doing this it was hoped to prevent the additional payments which had been concealed in these special orchestration fees as an inducement to favour the works of a particular publisher. The amount of money allowed under the agreement was, however, below current rates for such work, which meant that singers or orchestra leaders, unable to pay the extra money themselves, tended to rely on old songs with existing orchestrations or to use American songs with orchestrations supplied from the USA. Either way, the agreement militated against the successful launching of new British compositions. Recording companies too were not willing to pay for special orchestrations and tended to substitute American works with special orchestrations for new British compositions. Another feature of the agreement which angered composers was that any publisher found guilty of offering inducements might have his entire catalogue banned from broadcasting. Thus the composer could possibly have found his work and livelihood damaged because he happened to be represented in the banned catalogue. Composers were not alone in voicing their dislike of the agreement. Music Directors were also disturbed by the interference which the agreement entailed in their presentation of programmes. In exchange for dropping plugging payments, the Music Publishers' Association was now allowed to compile a list of current tunes from which Music Directors had to make up at least 60 per cent of their programmes.[2] Publishers, musicians,

1. Nor were music directors or artists consulted.
2. Report of the Committee on Broadcasting 1949, *op. cit.*, App. H, Paper 99 p.513.

show business entrepreneurs: all these groups seemed to be able to influence the BBC, but not the composers.[1]

The conclusion drawn from these events by popular and light composers, and by some other groups who were likewise dependent on the BBC for income and employment, was the simple but profoundly important one that many of these difficulties arose from 'the broadcasting monopoly'. Break the monopoly by providing an alternative broadcasting system and 'healthy competition'[2] would cure all. In 1951, when the Beveridge Report was published, this view found a place in a minority report by one of the Committee's members, Selwyn Lloyd. Unlike his colleagues, Lloyd could not agree that all the great influence that stemmed from the control of broadcasting should be 'vested in a public or a private monopoly',[3] or that the 'brute force of monopoly', which Lord Reith thought had enabled the BBC to follow a policy of 'moral responsibility', was free from danger.

The variety of attitudes amongst the seven groups[4] representing musical interests who submitted evidence to the Beveridge Committee over the monopoly question is worth examining. Four of the groups: the Composers' Guild, the National Association of Symphony Orchestras, the Incorporated Society of Musicians and the Performing Right Society offered no opinions about the BBC's broadcasting monopoly. The ISM and the PRS described their relations with the BBC as 'cordial' and 'friendly and harmonious' respectively.[5] The Composers' Guild thought the BBC was 'failing to do all it should in the propagation of our national heritage of music' and listed twelve specific criticisms. These included the preference for contemporary

1. The BBC's right to broadcast under its contract with the PRS was completely unrestricted as regards choice of works and number of broadcasting hours.
2. Report (etc.) 1949, App. H, Paper 99, p.513.
3. *Ibid.*, Cmnd. 8116, Minority Report, p.201.
4. They were: The Composers' Guild, the Songwriters' Guild, The Music Directors' Association, The Incorporated Society of Musicians, The National Association of Symphony Orchestras, The Musicians' Union, the Performing Right Society.
5. Report (etc.), App. H, Paper 100, p.514, and Paper 124, p.583.

works by foreign composers, insufficient opportunities for young composers, too few commissions for British composers and insufficient programme time for British contemporary music.[1] Two of the other groups came out strongly against the monopoly. The Songwriters' Guild wanted 'safeguards against the evils inherent in any form of monopoly' whilst the Music Directors' Association wanted the monopoly broken up. Only the Musicians' Union favoured 'the continued state ownership and management of broadcasting' and was against commercially sponsored broadcasting on the grounds that it would lower the quality of 'the product'.[2]

In the event, however, it was not in radio that the BBC first lost its monopoly but in television, and in 1955 under the supervision of a new public body, the Independent Television Authority, 'sponsored' programmes began to compete with the BBC's television service. Prior to the establishment of the ITA a large group of interested parties from the entertainment world, including the Songwriters' Guild, the Composers' Guild and the Musicians' Union, formed the Radio and Television Safeguards Committee. This alliance feared the effects likely to arise if American television, already commercially formidable, was able to undercut British programme contractors in supplying programme material. It might be said that the historical lesson to be drawn from the fate of the British film industry had been well learnt. Learning the lesson and translating it into legislative action were not the same thing, but due to the fact that no programmes could be created or transmitted without the co-operation of the members of the Safeguards Committee the group was in a strong position to secure legislative recognition of its demands. The result was that the Act creating the Independent Television Authority contained[3] a provision that the Authority should ensure that 'proper proportions of the recorded and other matter included in the programmes are of British origin and of British performance'. Although the

1. *Ibid.*, Paper 96, p.494.   2. *Ibid.*, Paper 102, p.515.
3. In Section 3(1)(*d*).

wording of this provision hardly amounted to a precise quantitative statement of the place of British material in independent television programmes, according to the historian of the Songwriters' Guild,[1] a convention was apparently reached by the mid-1960s that the 'proper' overall proportion of British material in independent television programmes should not be less than 85 per cent.[2]

Even if relationships with ITA were good, it nonetheless remained true that the amount of music required by the ITV companies was very much less than that used by the BBC. With one television and three radio channels (in 1959) controlled by the BBC, persuading the BBC to devote more time to British music remained the more important task. The rapid growth of record sales in the 1950s made the selection policy of the BBC's Gramophone Department of crucial importance to the popular songwriters. It was the Department which held 'the main key to the public ear'[3] and as such it gave little satisfaction to popular composers to find out in 1958, as a result of the Songwriters' Guild's programme monitoring, that the British proportion of output in the Gramophone Department's light and popular music programmes had fallen to 14·9 per cent. It was not pure facetiousness for the Guild to enquire whether the BBC had indeed become 'the Voice of America',[4] for the American music industry appeared to be insurmountably strong in the popular music market at the end of the 1950s. This dominance was however to be strongly challenged in the following decade.

Increasing the demand for their members' services and replacing music imports were not the only activities of the Guilds

1. See, The Songwriters' Guild of Great Britain, *op. cit.*, pp.19–20.
2. It must be said that this statement about the satisfactory position of British music in ITV differs from the evidence of the Songwriters' Guild to the Pilkington Committee (see Report of the Committee on Broadcasting, 1960, Vol. II, App. E, Paper No. 135, pp.807–11) where it was stated that the Authority was 'failing in its duty' to implement Section 3(1)(*d*) and where the Guild argued that 'A foreign quota, or set of quotas, binding upon all broadcasting organizations, must be fixed with the utmost precision, and by Statute.'
3. The Songwriters' Guild of Great Britain, *op. cit.*, p.30.
4. *Ibid.*, p.31.

during the 1950s. Both sought to establish standard contracts which their members could use as a basis for negotiations with publishers. Despite an abortive attempt at amalgamation, mutual harmony between the two Guilds was still sufficiently strong to enable them to pursue their common interests through a Joint Consultative Committee[1] in alliance with the Arrangers, Composers and Copyists section of the Musicians' Union. One such common interest arose over the attempt by a group of film producers to demand a share of composers' performing fees when negotiating contracts for film music. Although no universally acceptable film music contract could be negotiated, the film producers did agree to withdraw their claim for a share of performing fees.[2] In matters of public policy too, such as the enquiry into the law of copyright which began in April, 1951, composers found representation through their Guilds.

Popular Music 1951–70

By 1951 'the Age of Austerity'[3] was well nigh over. As food rationing ended and economic controls were relaxed welfare-state Britain moved into an era of unprecedented material prosperity. Affluence replaced austerity. Mid-century British society enjoyed virtual full employment, growing incomes and increased leisure. It was an urban society and one more consciously egalitarian than before the war. Its success was highly dependent on exploiting new forms of technology. Its members were mobile. It was a society in which economic affluence ran hand in hand with relaxed social controls and in which fashion and novelty became ends in themselves. Music influenced and was in turn influenced by these developments. This was especially true of popular music.

During the 1950s the whole character of popular music

1. *Ibid.*, p.16.
2. *Ibid.*, p.19.
3. After M. Sissons and P. French (eds.), *The Age of Austerity 1945–51*, London, 1959.

changed completely. Musical taste, especially among the young, moved away from the 'swing' music of the large orchestra to the music of the small 'group'. The original impetus for this change was partly economic and partly technological: the high fees charged by large orchestras of as many as twenty pieces made them expensive to employ for all but the largest engagement, whilst technological improvements in amplifying equipment meant that the same volume of sound could be produced by fewer musicians. Although the big bands had enjoyed popular following the important thing about the small group was that its very smallness enabled 'the fans' to identify themselves with its individual members.

Whilst swing music did not entirely disappear, popular music split into several component parts. The jazz music of the 1930s gave way in the 1950s to traditional (trad) jazz. Dance music, the old-fashioned type of swing music, steadily lost its popularity but retained a small, loyal following. None of the developments in these two areas of popular music matched the rapid changes in the third category: the creation of a music style specifically designed for the young. Commercially, what made the teenage market important was its high disposable income. Full employment, the narrowing of the differential between adult and apprentice rates of pay, and the absence of family responsibilities: all these meant that teenagers in the 1950s and 1960s had more money to spend than ever before. Unlike popular music before the war, which tended to find a market amongst a wide variety of ages, incomes and social standing, the new music catered for a special teenage public with its own tastes and styles. By the end of the 1950s the musical press reflected this change. The top twenty lists were no longer based on sheet music sales but on record sales, and the tunes appearing in the hit parade were the ones which fed the teenage market.[1] Teenagers became the biggest buyers of 'pop' records. Their spending power controlled over 40 per cent of the record

1. A. Bicat, 'Fifties Children: Sixties People', in V. Bognador, and R. Skidelsky, *The Age of Affluence*.

market by 1959[1] and formed the largest single identifiable market.

The teenagers were not just listeners. The rock' n' roll mania which, with 'its non-electronic shadow', skiffle,[2] swept over the country in 1956, extended the popularity of semi-amateur music making over a much wider and predominantly younger section of the population than had ever been covered by the older style pop music. The instrumentation of the pop groups was also different. In place of the saxophone of the swing bands came the electric guitar with its battery of amplification equipment. Skiffle, on the other hand, tended to eschew technology's offerings. It spread its message by means of guitar, washboard, tea-chest (plus broom handle and string). Nor, for those groups who sought to earn a living by the new music, was a high level of professional musical competence necessary. Anyone with a minimum of musical ability could participate in skiffle. It was doubtful too whether a polished musical performance was what the fans wanted. As highly valued were 'the pelvic gyration' and 'the rhythm'.

The new music did not amount to the reappearance of a particularly British popular music idiom. Rock 'n' roll, skiffle and rhythm and blues all came out of America. The most successful British exponents of the new music were imitators of American idols so that the new music enhanced rather than countered the dominance of American commercial interests in the pop music market. This dominance was reflected both in the high sales of recordings by American artists and in the large proportion of American music used in broadcasting. The closing years of the 1950s were however the high water mark of American success in the British pop market. In the next decade British popular music staged a breakthrough. How did this come about? The historian of the Songwriters' Guild attributes the breakthrough[3]

1. *Ibid.*
2. C. Booker, *The Neophiliacs*, London, 1969, p.38. Nevertheless, the 'pop music' craze has permeated all sections of the population, so that the 'hit parade', the list of top selling records, is now regularly published in serious journals.
3. The Songwriters' Guild of Great Britain, *op. cit.*, p.31.

to its successful campaign in 1959 that was aimed at increasing the proportion of British material used by the BBC's Gramophone Department. Whilst this was undoubtedly a factor of some importance, given the interdependence of the two media, it was not sufficient by itself to guarantee the success of British pop music in the sixties. The weakness of British pop music between 1945 and 1959 could not simply be blamed on the media. Rather it lay in the nature of the work being produced by British popular composers. This was touched on incidentally by the Songwriters' Guild in a memorandum to the BBC in 1947[1]: 'and if there is one criticism we would make of the BBC itself it is that there exists, among the younger and less experienced of its producers, a tendency to favour "transatlantic" entertainment as being more cosmopolitan and less "corny" (if we may be forgiven the term) than the home grown product.'

'More cosmopolitan and less corny than the home grown product': here in a phrase was an accurate diagnosis of the ills of British popular music. British pop music failed, at least until the mid-1950s, to catch the popular mood, especially the mood of the young. British popular music was 'square'. It wasn't 'hep' or in 'the groove' – to borrow contemporary catch words which themselves had been borrowed by British teenagers from across the Atlantic.[2] Imitation may well be the sincerest form of flattery but it did not help the creation of a distinctively British popular music idiom.

It was through affluence that the music market expanded in the 1950s. But affluence, the young soon came to realize, was not an end in itself. The mood of disillusionment and disenchantment amongst teenagers with the British version of the 'Affluent Society' helped to create a new music idiom. The Beatles were the first to tap this mood but the 'pop explosion' of the early 1960s which carried record sales to a peak in 1964 brought many groups in its train. It was not music which was peculiarly British. On the contrary, what was significant was that the new

1. *Ibid.*, p.25.
2. C. Booker, *op. cit.*, p.38.

music was internationally acceptable and successful. In March 1964, for example, American advance sales for the Beatles sixth record 'Can't buy me love' were two million, a record still unbroken.[1] More was to follow, and the following month: 'They commanded not only the first five places in the American Top 100 but also the first two places in the LP charts; and that in a year in which America, like England was enjoying its biggest record boom in history.' Nor, as has been argued, was it a development altogether lacking in irony: 'It was the first time that any country had fought back against America's domination of twentieth-century mass culture since the first craze for "Alexander's Ragtime Band" in 1912. And the irony of it was, of course, that America's rout had been achieved with what were almost entirely her own weapons.'[2]

The boom in British pop music sparked off by the Beatles was not without its own ludicrous features. The Beatles were variously described as 'the greatest composers since Beethoven' and 'our best export'. They in turn claimed to be 'more popular than Jesus now'.[3] Still, where they led others followed and the progression of groups through the pop music market continues apparently unabated. The style of pop music and of the performers has, however, changed. If the Beatles were not entirely acceptable to the older generation their music could at least be made into arrangements which could bridge 'the generation gap'.[4] This is not so true of most recent developments in pop music. The music of protest and revolt, of the drug culture, of bewilderment and disillusionment with the Affluent Society, has made 'the pop song a battlefield between the young and the old, between them and us'.[5]

1. *Ibid.*
2. *Ibid.*
3. Quoted in C. Booker, *op. cit.*, at pages 221, 235 and 262. The opinion that the Beatles were 'the greatest composers since Beethoven' was expressed by Richard Buckle, music critic of the *Sunday Times*, 29 December 1963.
4. It is doubtful how successful such adaptations have been as the basic material depends strongly on the style of expression of the group.
5. A. Bicat, *op. cit.*, p.327–8.

The Performing Right 1939–70

In 1939 the Performing Right Society could look back on twenty-five years of solid achievement. It had a membership which covered the entire music publishing industry. It represented a large number of foreign collecting societies and, where no collecting society existed, agents had been established to protect members' interests. Unity in membership was matched by a much wider recognition amongst music users of the performing right. In its defence of the right, the Society had undertaken a large amount of pioneer litigation as well as countering potentially damaging legislation. In the last year before the Second World War the Society had collected over £600,000 in revenue from over 40,000 licensees. Administrative expenses amounted to little more than 10 per cent of the total revenue and the administrative achievement in 'policing' the performing right and collecting and distributing this money was considerable, even if camouflaged by the routine nature which the operation now began to assume. Only one outstanding problem hung over the Society and this was the monopoly issue.

1939–45 The problems faced by the Society during the war were not dissimilar from those which affected other large business organizations. The shortage of manpower, the loss of employees for military service and the dispersal of records were countered by longer working hours, a simplified basis for distribution, increased office mechanization and agreements with major music users, such as the BBC, to stabilize payments during the war. Although initially the Society's revenue was hit by the closure of places of entertainment, several new markets developed during the war. The most important of these involved the use of music in factories. Despite the deliberately low tariff which was set by the Society, the right to collect fees for performances in factories was challenged by industrial interests. In a test case instituted by the Society against Gillette Industries Ltd (1943) it was held that music provided for workpeople in factories was a performance in public for the purposes of the Copyright Act 1911. Besides this further judicial interpretation of what constituted a public performance the publicity surrounding the case led to a general agreement between the Society and the Treasury covering the use of music 'in practically every factory in the United Kingdom'.[1]

One particular problem arising out of the war was the question of the Society's collection of royalties on enemy-owned copyright. After the outbreak of war the Patents, Designs, Copyright and Trade Marks (Emergency) Act 1939 was passed by Parliament, providing, inter alia, that a licence granted to a person resident in the United Kingdom in respect of an enemy-owned copyright would not be invalid despite the Trading with the Enemy Act 1939. Further, copyright was not withdrawn from works originating in enemy countries. Thus the Society continued to control in the UK the repertoire of its affiliated societies in the countries with which the UK was at war, although the royalties collected by it in respect of these repertoires were payable to the Custodian of Enemy Property pending an international settlement on the conclusion of peace treaties. Similar provisions were made in the legislation of enemy countries. For the duration of the war, however, the Society's foreign income was limited to that from the non-belligerent countries of Europe and those in the American and Australian continents, while only its agencies operating outside the areas of hostilities could continue to function. Not until some ten years after the cessation of hostilities was the last of these blocked accounts released.

1945–56 Although by 1945 the Society had both a higher membership (2,062 compared to 1,861 in 1939) and revenue (£858,000 compared to £595,000 in 1939) the Society was faced with a rich legacy of problems as a result of the war. The most serious related to tariffs. Despite the increase in the Society's money income during the war the real distribution per

1. C. F. James, *op. cit.*, p.100.

member in 1945 was far below the immediate pre-war level. In part this was a direct result of the stabilization agreements negotiated during the war, but another factor was also responsible: rising prices. During the 1930s the price of most commodities fell and the task of achieving increases in real income for members was a relatively easy one, though in particular years, e.g. 1926, when there was a large increase in membership, new and higher tariffs had to be negotiated quickly to maintain the level of distributions. Between 1939 and 1945, however, as prices rose, very few tariff negotiations took place except when new licensing agreements were established. In the pre-war economic situation tariffs had not been designed to cope with rising prices, with the inevitable result that as the price level continued to drift upwards after 1945 it became increasingly difficult to maintain members' real distributions. Realizing the unsatisfactory basis for its tariffs the Society set about re-negotiating old established licensing arrangements immediately the war ended. Despite a substantial number of successful negotiations it was not until 1954 that the Society was able to reach a level of real distribution higher than in the peak inter-war year of 1937. In Chapter 3 it was pointed out that one general problem concerning tariffs had been the high costs involved in negotiations. So long as tariffs lacked an automatic adjustment mechanism to take into account changes in the price level, tariffs had to be revised frequently. Revisions both increased the Society's costs and antagonized music users. Their dislike of upward revisions was to play an important part in the revived discussion of the Society's monopoly powers in the early 1950s.

Revision of the Law of Copyright The 1909 Committee on Copyright, whose enquiry resulted in the Copyright Act of 1911, found the law of copyright in what they described as 'a state of confusion'.[1] Their recommendation that action should be taken 'to place British law on an intelligible and systematic footing' was accomplished in no small measure by the 1911 Act.

1. Report of the Copyright Committee, 1952, Cmnd. 8662 (Preliminary).

When that Act was passed, the cinema was barely established, the record manufacturers described themselves as belonging to 'an infant industry'[1] and there was no radio or television. By 1951 these 'spectacular developments in the technical field' made some of the provisions of the 1911 Act look 'somewhat outdated'.[2]

Technological change was not the only factor which made examination of British copyright law a matter of urgency. The 1911 Act had followed and embodied the general provisions of the original Berne Convention (1886) as revised at Berlin in 1908. Since 1911 there had been two further International Conventions of the Berne Union. The first, the Rome Convention of 1928, did not lead to any alterations in the 1911 Act but the second, the Brussels Convention of 1948, did. Two of the amendments to the International Copyright Convention agreed on at Brussels concerned the performing right. These related to Articles 11 (performing right) and 11 (*bis*) (broadcasting). The revised form of Article 11 conferred an *exclusive* right upon the author to authorize the public performance of his works. The article was brought into line with other rights which had already been defined in the Convention as exclusive. The effect of the revision of Article 11 (*bis*) was to amplify the exclusive rights of the author in regard to the broadcasting of his works including the re-transmission of broadcasts or their relay by means of loudspeakers or television sets. As such, it added to the protection necessary for the composer in the face of technological change and was generally welcome. However, the revision also carried with it the provision that countries of the Berne Union could determine the conditions under which these rights might be exercised and also the author's remuneration in respect of them in the absence of agreement. This provision was made to apply to the performing right as well. It was accompanied by a declaration from the UK delegation to the effect that: '. . . His Majesty's Government remain free to enact such legislation as

1. Report of the Copyright Committee, 1909.
2. Report of the Copyright Committee, 1952 (Preliminary).

may be considered necessary in the public interest to prevent or deal with any abuse of the monopoly rights conferred upon copyright owners by United Kingdom law.'[1]

As was discussed (in page 78 above) the issue of dealing with any abuse of monopoly rights was raised during the investigation into the 'Tuppenny Bill' in 1929. The Select Committee had suggested then that music users should have '. . . a right of appeal to an independent body when they are faced with unreasonable demands, and are unable to come to a mutually satisfactory agreement with the Society'.[2] The Committee proposed a tribunal or arbitration, but recognizing that this was contrary to the terms of the 1908 Berlin Convention suggested that the Board of Trade frame a policy to secure a change in the convention. A Departmental Committee on International Copyright appointed in 1935 formulated a provision which was almost exactly that adopted at Brussels in 1948: an addition to Article II empowering any member of the Berne Union to regulate the performing right when the right was owned or controlled by one association 'if it is able to, and *does* impose unduly onerous charges or exercise its right unreasonably'. At the same time the 1935 Committee stated that no substantial grounds for complaint about the way in which the performing right was exercised in Britain existed and that the proposed addition to Article II should not be taken to imply that protective legislation was now necessary. There matters rested until the Brussels Convention when Article II was revised. Even after the amendment was made, however, the then President of the Board of Trade, Mr Harold Wilson, could tell the PRS that the declaration on monopoly abuse had been made:

. . not because there is any evidence at all of necessity for the alteration, but because it was essential to preserve the position if, at some later date, there should ever be legislation to control the rate of royalties. I have received as yet no such evidence. I think this Society

1. Quoted in C. F. James, *op. cit.*, p.117.
2. Special Report (etc.) 1930, *op. cit.*, at p.vi.

has followed a policy for the past twenty years or more which has been, in my view, of the very highest national interest.[1]

While the Board of Trade was building up the government's defences to deal with an abuse for which, according to its statements, no evidence existed, the PRS was continuing the process of revising the Society's tariffs to bring them into line with post-war conditions. In doing so the Society ran into considerable opposition from some music users. The degree of opposition encountered seems to have been related to two factors; the age of the existing tariff and the economic position of the music user. Because of the gap in tariff renewals caused by the war, some of the agreements re-negotiated in the latter half of the 1940s dated back to the 1920s. To bring them up to a realistic level they had to be increased considerably. For example, the cinema tariff which was re-negotiated in 1947 was thirteen years old, and the music hall tariff was even older as it had not been revised since 1929. Both these forms of entertainment had begun to experience competition from other media such as television and records, and it was felt that the Society's tariffs should take account of these changes in their economic circumstances. On the other hand, declining profitability tended to be unevenly spread, for some users were still quite profitable and the PRS saw no reason why composers should accept lower fees all round. Well aware of the growing resistance amongst music users to its tariff revision programme it was made clear in 1946 that:

. . . a Society such as ours, representing as it now does almost the whole of the world's composers, cannot by reason of the very strength it holds, exercise its powers in an arbitrary manner. We should not seek to be the sole judges of the value of our own rights, but should agree upon this by negotiation, and if that fails we should submit the matter to arbitration.[2]

Despite the offer of arbitration, no music user (with the sole exception of the BBC in 1937) agreed to it, and the PRS was left

1. Quoted in C. F. James, *op. cit.*, p.118.
2. See *Performing Right*, 1946.

to impose its new tariffs unilaterally in cases of failure in attempts to reach agreement.

New technological developments, changes in the International Copyright Convention and resistance to tariff increases: these were the background to the appointment of the Copyright Committee in April, 1951. So far as the performing right was concerned the Committee discussed three main questions:

a   whether the right of public performance as hitherto enjoyed and as interpreted in the Courts is unreasonably wide or has been exercised in a manner prejudicial to the public interest;

b   whether rights akin to the rights of public performances ought to be created or (where they already exist) be continued in respect of the public representation of material which is not copyright material in the usual sense, e.g. sporting events, broadcast programmes, gramophone records and the characteristic rendering of works by performers; and

c   if and in as far as such rights should be conferred whether they should be as extensive as those enjoyed by copyright owners in respect of the public performance of copyright works.[1]

Questions *b* and *c* covered the issue of ancillary rights which broadcasters and professional sports promoters were hoping would protect their commercial interests. Broadcasting authorities were given the right to prevent the copying of their programmes but only in television and the Report emphasized that this right as well as the public performance right in records was to be regarded as ancillary to the primary rights of composers and authors.

As the principal innovation in the 1956 Copyright Act resulting from the Committee's Report was the establishment of the Performing Right Tribunal it is worth examining the investigation into question *a*. In its Report the Committee stated that it had '... been faced with a large volume of criticism from many quarters directed at the way in which rights of public performance are exercised. The evidence leaves us little doubt that this criticism is not without its justification'.[2] After deciding that the PRS con-

1. Report (etc.) 1952, *op. cit.*, at para. 123.   2. *Ibid.*, at para. 122.

stituted a monopoly, despite the existence of non-copyright music in the public domain, the Committee discussed the criticisms made by music users about the Society's operations. Their main one was '. . . the arbitrary manner in which the Society has established its various tariffs and the arbitrary way . . . these . . . have altered from time to time.'[1] Its origin lay in the post-war upward revision of tariffs. Despite the government's earlier reservations about lack of evidence of monopoly abuse it is surprising that at no time during the Committee's proceedings was any attempt made to investigate the effects on licensees of the changes in tariff rates which music users were complaining about. Standards of proof seemed to vary between the Society and the music user. The abnormally strong bargaining position of the Society, given its control over practically all popular music and the absence of any statutory obligation on the Society to submit any of its tariffs to arbitration were the main reasons music users wished 'some form of standing tribunal to which they would have a statutory right of appeal'.[2]

The music users' most severe criticism was not directed at the Performing Right Society but was reserved for Phonographic Performance Ltd for its power 'threatened and exercised, to withhold licences at discretion'.[3] The almost accidental nature of the origin of the right to control the public performance of re-cords,[4] the arbitrary manner in which the rates were fixed, and the withholding of licences 'for reasons which are remote from any question of copyright'[5] forced the Committee to the conclusion '. . . that the rights given have been enforced in an arbitrary and autocratic manner, with the minimum of consideration and . . . that . . . some way must be found of limiting by statute, the opportunities of exploitation flowing from the present interpretation of the term "public performance" in this connection'.[6]

1. *Ibid.*, at para. 138.   2. *Ibid.*, at para. 139.
3. *Ibid.*, at para. 148.
4. *Ibid.*, at paras. 140–6.
5. *Ibid.*, at para. 149.   6. *Ibid.*, at para. 150.

Despite this harsh criticism the Committee did recognize that Phonographic Performance Ltd, was not acting as an independent agent but was constrained by its relationship with the Musicians' Union. With the improvement in the quality of records, their use for public performances seemed to be a real threat to the employment of musicians, and the Musicians' Union regarded the imposition of fees for the public performance of records and the restrictions on their use as a means of safeguarding members' interests. Other groups from within the music industry in addition to music users voiced opposition to the way in which the public performance right in records was exercised. The PRS, the Songwriters' Guild, and the Music Publishers' Association opposed it because by preventing the public performance of music it vitally affected the earnings of composers and lyric writers.

The Committee's conclusions about the operations of the collecting societies had some important results. In considering the claims by other interests, such as the BBC, the Sports Promoters, the Musicians' Union, Equity and the Variety Artists Federation for the creation of additional performing rights the Committee was influenced by the experience in the exercise of the established rights. Thus it recognized that any new rights would be cumulative so that if the BBC received a right to control public performances of its broadcasts then '. . . for an event like the Lord Mayor's Show, the incidental performance of a piece of copyright music by a band in the course of the procession would attract three separate licences. The refusal by any one of the licensors would mean that the wireless set remained dumb'.[1] It also emphasized that the new rights which it recommended in television broadcasting and those which it proposed should be confirmed in gramophone records should be subsidiary to the primary right of the composer or author of a copyright work reproduced by television or recording, and that the rights in television programmes or records should be without prejudice to the

1. *Ibid.*, at para. 177.

primary right.[1] Lastly, the Committee sought a solution to 'the fundamental problem . . . of how to secure for the general public the maximum benefits of these scientific and technical developments, while at the same time providing adequate protection for those who make these benefits possible'.[2] The form of its solution took was to recommend that a tribunal be appointed

a   to review and revise tariffs actually in operation, both as to the class of entertainment covered by a tariff and the fees chargeable thereunder;

b   to make new tariffs where none exist or where the scope of any existing tariff seems to them to be inappropriate; and

c   to determine whether or not refusals to grant licences (or whether any conditions attached to licences issued) are detrimental to the public interest, and if so to grant licences of right, subject to such conditions as the Tribunal may decide.[3]

With the establishment of the Performing Right Tribunal under the Copyright Act of 1956 the collecting societies lost their unrestricted rights to control and prevent the use of copyrights material for public performance. From 1956 all tariffs had to be constructed with the possibility of review by the Tribunal in mind.[4]

With the publication of the Report of the Copyright Committee in October 1952 the PRS became involved in a struggle over the ensuing legislation in Parliament. The creation of the Tribunal was the most important new feature of the Copyright Bill but there were also others which seemed detrimental to

1. The effect of granting concurrent performing and broadcasting rights to authors and publishers, on the one hand, and record manufacturers, on the other, is nevertheless necessarily to make the former subservient to the latter regarding 'needle time'. This question is discussed in greater detail in R. F. Whale, *Copyright, Evolution, Theory and Practice*, London, 1971, at Chapter 5.
2. *Report* (etc.) *1952*, at para. 210.
3. *Ibid.*, at para. 179.
4. One substantial advantage gained by the PRS from the existence of the Performing Right Tribunal is shelter from the too easy accusation of 'monopoly abuse'.

members' interests and which at the time involved substantial negotiations. Two features of the Committee's recommendations may serve as examples of the efforts of the Society in preventing the narrowing of members' rights. One cause for anxiety was the recommendation that, in the absence of express agreement to the contrary, the copyright in any work created for valuable consideration in pursuance of an agreement to create it should vest in the person giving the commission. Although the Committee coupled this recommendation with the proviso that the author should nevertheless have the right to restrain the use of the work for any other purpose than that for which it had been created, it failed to appreciate that this wide extension of the already existing exceptions to the basic rule that the creator of a work is the first owner of the copyright in his creation was to strike at the foundations of the author's right. One effect of this recommendation, had it been fully implemented, would have been that the copyright in nearly all music specially commissioned for films would have vested automatically in the film producer, for the possibility that the composer would have been able to reserve his performing right in such circumstances would have been remote. Although this recommendation was partially implemented in the Act, the Society's representations, together with those of the British Copyright Council, secured the exemption of music from the relevant provisions and the restriction in the cases of literary, dramatic and artistic works to those of employee authors. The importance of these modifications has since become very evident with the great increase in the commissioning of works, particularly for television and radio. Another feature of the Bill, damaging to composers' interests, was the clause giving the Tribunal power to exempt, wholly or partially, from liability to the performing right, of clubs, societies or organizations not established or conducted for profit, but 'whose main objects are charitable or otherwise concerned with the advancement of religion, education or social welfare'. This provision was so wide it was at first feared it might cover the BBC itself, but it has not, in fact, been so interpreted. The exemption

secured by the PRS for its members' rights, as distinct from
those of the broadcasters and record manufacturers, which remain within the ambit of the relevant provisions of the Act, may
have been due in part to recognition of the Society's practice of
making only nominal charges to such voluntary organizations as
the Boy Scouts, Youth Clubs, the YMCA and YWCA and to giving a free licence in the cases of charitable performances where
the performers also give their services without charge.

In addition to emerging from 'the Battle of the Copyright
Bill' with several important amendments to it the Performing
Right Society had also established links with other organizations
representing copyright owners and in March, 1953, there was
formed the British Joint Copyright Council. This concentrated
the efforts of all the creative copyright owners in defence of
their rights and provided an authoritative medium for negotiations with the authorities on behalf of such owners generally.
It thus continued one of the features of the post-war copyright
world: the tendency for specialized pressure groups to be created
to guard copyright owners' interests. From the music industry
the British Joint Copyright Council drew support from the Performing Right Society, the Mechanical Rights Society, the
Music Publishers' Association and the Composers' Guild. The
main justification for the Council's existence was the fight over
the Copyright Bill, but with the likely continuation of copyright
problems as a result of changes in technology and in international law the Council survived the passing of the 1956 Act.
In 1965 the Council decided to widen its representation by increasing its membership and to develop its activities by taking
on 'educational' work to promote a wider understanding of copyright and its attendant problems. Reconstituted as the British
Copyright Council, under the chairmanship of the late Sir Alan
Herbert, it pressed the government during the 1960s to take
action over such matters as the pop music pirates, the International Copyright Convention revisions of 1971 and the public
lending right for authors. It has also published several booklets
on copyright problems.

With the creation of the Songwriters' Guild and the Composers' Guild it could be said that a greater degree of division of labour had taken place in the protection of composers' interests. One motive for forming these societies had been recognition of the fact that there were certain policy questions which the PRS could not take up because of its international obligations. One such issue was the question of attaching conditions to the PRS licence as a means of securing the use of more British music. In 1962 this proposal came to the surface again. This time it took the form of a demand that every licence which the Society issued to the BBC and the programme contractor to ITA should include a condition that a specified quota of British music must be broadcast. As in the 1930s, the Society could only reject these moves to impose limitations on the licensees' free choice and it emphasized that:

As individuals we can join the British Songwriters' Guild, the Composers' Guild and the Music Publishers' Association, but *as a Society* we are bound by our contracts with all the other societies collecting composers' performing right royalties on conditions that absolutely forbid discrimination against any affiliated society, nothing but disaster could follow any attempt by the Society to impose a quota upon its licences.[1]

In reality, the conflict of interest which the quota proposal involved was not between the members and the Society but rather between composers and publishers. For a while around 1961 the composers used the annual general meetings of the Society as a platform for voicing their discontent about what they considered to be a lack of eagerness on the part of music publishers to exploit British material. With the pop explosion of 1963–4 and the growth in the popularity of British music abroad, these complaints evaporated.

In evidence to the Copyright Committee the PRS stated that in 1950 it had issued over 50,000 licences. Fifteen years later the Society had almost 100,000 licensees in the UK and this repre-

1. *Performing Right*, 1962.

sented a rate of growth far higher than that experienced pre-war. The new markets for music were many. Some were simply replacements for old-established forms of entertainment that had succumbed to new competition. For example, with the post-war slump in the cinema and the music hall the Society had lost a large number of worthwhile licences but this loss was in some degree compensated for by the use of music at bingo sessions. The demise of the small variety theatre was compensated for by the increased royalty income from the resurgence in working men's clubs in the North and Midlands. By far the largest expansion came about as a result of improved mechanical means of musical reproduction. The 'coin-operated phonograph' or jukebox, an experiment in the 1930s, proliferated after the Second World War and by 1960 the Society had licensed 8,000 of them. Like the development of trouble-free background music systems which spread into aircraft, motor coaches, bowling alleys, and supermarkets, the jukebox was important because it expanded the licensing field as businesses such as small cafés and restaurants installed them, but the biggest expansion in this field occurred when they were taken up by the big brewery companies, with their thousands of outlets, after the relaxation of the licensing laws regarding music in public houses. Expansion in the composers' market was not just dependent on technological advance. The Betting and Gaming Act of 1960 opened the way to a large increase in the numbers of gaming clubs and with background music another new market appeared.

It is fair to say that although the income from these new sources of revenue is a very substantial item in the Society's revenue the phenomenon of background music is regretted by many of its members as a perversion of music's purpose and art. In fact background music in its original conception as an unobtrusive instrumental accompaniment to monotonous work or to re-creation (or even to strenuous mental activity, for it has been proved that music has considerable therapeutic value) is, as many people will agree, a valuable discovery.

As first applied by them, it was accepted among suppliers of background music, that unobtrusiveness was essential, so much so that it was desirable to use specially composed music rather than familiar works. Unfortunately, in these members' eyes, the original idea has been crudely exploited, the vibrant amplification of jukebox recordings now frequently replacing the carefully selected and appropriately modulated 'piped music' of the first concept, so that 'background music', at least since the 'beat' era, has renounced its original function and become an extension of the all-pervading 'pop scene' – a sort of continuous pop festival, heartbreaking to anyone with a sensitive appreciation of music, even if that appreciation extends, as it often does, to the better areas of the pop field. Perhaps the most striking development in the last decade has occurred, not in the UK, but overseas. The remarkable conquest of overseas markets by British pop music has led as can be seen from table 4.3 to income from overseas agencies and affiliated societies becoming the largest single source of income, even greater than the revenue from broadcasting which had dominated until 1965. The PRS, in its reciprocal accountings with its foreign affiliated societies, had nearly always had a favourable 'balance of payments' with those societies, in spite of an unfavourable balance with the United States of America in particular. When that balance swung in favour of the Society even in the USA the overall surplus enjoyed by the Society was of the order of 2 million pounds (1970), bringing the Society the Queen's Award to Industry for services to 'invisible exports'.

International Copyright　One reflection of the changing sources of the Society's income, especially the increasing importance of revenue from overseas, has been the attention paid by the Society to international copyright. International copyright is concerned with treaties or conventions between nations requiring the signatories to respect, in their own countries, the copyrights of nationals of other signatories. There is no general principle of international law which requires such protection so it is to international convention and treaties that the copyright

Table 4.3 The Performing Right Society Ltd – Summary of Income 1915–70
(All £000)

	Domestic		Overseas agencies	Affiliated societies	Interest etc.	Total
	General	Broadcasting				
1915	4·1					4·1
1920	22·5					22·5
1925	42·9					42·9
1930	113·1 (65%)	60·3 (35%)				173·4
1935	153·1 (44%)	134·7 (39%)	19·4 (6%)	32·2 (9%)	6·9 (2%)	346·3
1940	175·3 (28%)	337·0 (54%)	54·8 (9%)	33·6 (5%)	18·4 (3%)	619·1
1945	316·1 (37%)	419·5 (49%)	61·0 (7%)	40·0 (5%)	21·4 (2%)	858·0
1950	481·6 (32%)	636·1 (43%)	78·2 (5%)	269·7 (18%)	29·0 (2%)	1,494·6
1955	583·5 (24%)	902·6 (37%)	152·3 (6%)	747·0 (31%)	58·3 (2%)	2,443·7
1960	880·3 (27%)	1,452·8 (44%)	210·8 (6%)	660·8 (20%)	90·8 (3%)	3,295·5
1965	1,527·2 (27%)	1,960·8 (35%)	217·6 (4%)	1,748·2 (31%)	162·8 (3%)	5,611·6
1970	2,385·8 (26%)	2,605·7 (28%)	283·9 (4%)	3,601 (39%)	250·9 (3%)	9,127·4

owner must look for protection. Although in some countries such conventions and treaties are regarded by the courts as part of the law of the land, this is not so in the UK,[1] but as has been discussed (see pp. 49, 129), British copyright law has tended to move in line with international conventions. The Berne Copyright Union was set up in 1886 and the States which joined it undertook to grant the protection of their national copyright laws to works originating in other States members of the Union. It was also agreed that the member States should in their own national copyright laws conform to the standards specified in the conventions of the Union. The countries belonging to the Berne Copyright Union conceived of copyright as a right which on grounds of equity naturally – and therefore without the fulfilment of formalities – to the creators of literary, dramatic, musical and artistic works.[2] As such the Berne Copyright Union developed during the first half of the twentieth century into the most important and widely accepted system of international copyright. It did suffer, however, from the disadvantage that a number of countries, particularly those in the Western Hemisphere, including the USA, who favoured the stipulation of formalities for the acquisition of copyright were not to adhere to it. As the barriers to international communication fell in the face of technological advance the inconvenience arising from the diversity of copyright systems became increasingly evident and in 1952 an attempt was made to secure a universally acceptable copyright convention. The attempt to bridge two different conceptions of copyright: the Berne conception that the creator's copyright in his work is an exclusive and natural right which comes into existence with the act of creation, although the state may limit it in certain directions, and the opposing view that copyright is a privilege accorded by the state on certain conditions, was a project not without risk. It carried the dangerous possibility that the conditions necessary to secure the adherence

1. See Copinger and Skone James, *op. cit.*, para. 1101.
2. See R. F. Whale, 'The Universal Copyright Convention', *Performing Right*, September 1955.

of both groups might result in the debasement of the high standards enjoyed by authors in Berne Union countries. Although not immediately apparent this proved to be the case. Under the Universal Copyright Convention of 1952 each contracting state undertook to give the unpublished works of the nationals of all other contracting States the same protection as it gave to the works of its own nationals. Its main advance was to give protection to works published outside a state without the necessity for formalities.[1] The period of copyright protection – the life of the author and twenty-five years after his death – was lower than that afforded by the Berne Union. It established minimum levels of protection but these were far below the Berne levels. In effect it left the mode and extent of protection to the separate legislation of each state. In only one area did protection extend further than the Berne convention: it required protection to be given to published works, not only if first published in a contracting state, but if first published anywhere, if the author was a national of a contracting state.[2]

So long as individual countries maintained higher standards of protection the fact that the Universal Copyright Convention had substantially lower standards was not immediately alarming. However, with the process of de-colonization, newly independent nations began to throw off the legal systems of their imperial rulers. As countries which were net importers from the point of view of copyright material, usually with severe overall shortages of foreign exchange and lacking substantial copyright owning interests, the trend which emerged was one of diminished copyright protection. Ghana for example, the first of the independent black African states in its Copyright Act of 1961

1. Except that copies were to bear the symbol © accompanied by the name of the copyright proprietor and the year of first publication. See Copinger and Skone James, *op. cit.*, paras. 1147–52.
2. This position is now appreciably modified under the provisions of the Berne and Universal Conventions as revised at Paris in 1971. For a detailed exposition of the changes then made, including the special concessions made to the 'developing countries', see R. F. Whale, *Copyright Evolution, Theory, and Practice*, London, 1972.

reduced its protection of the author's right to the barest minimum. It left the Berne Copyright Union, of which it had been a member, and adhered only to the Universal Copyright Convention with its very few specific obligations.

A period now ensued when it seemed quite possible that the international copyright protection system would break down. The emergency itself, however, produced a remedy. After a series of international conferences at governmental level a 'package deal', as it was called, was reached between the developing countries, on the one hand, and the developed countries, on the other, in which the former were granted certain advantages under both international conventions and which were incorporated in the revised texts drawn up in 1971 (see note p. 143).

Nevertheless, the musical copyright seems particularly vulnerable, although it is outside the scope of the concessions made to the developing countries, because of the ease with which it is possible to apply a restrictive definition to the concept of public performance where performances are as ubiquitous as in the case of musical works.

Confusion in international copyright during the 1960s was matched at home by the confusion arising from the actions of the Performing Right Tribunal. Despite its parentage in the reservation to the 1948 Berne Convention about enacting legislation to 'deal with any abuse of monopoly rights' the Tribunal's powers were not limited to the restraint of abuse but directed to solving disputes and making orders 'as the Tribunal may determine to be reasonable in the circumstances'. This still left the old problem of establishing criteria to test what was 'reasonable'. It meant that neither music user nor licensing body could construct its case with any degree of certainty as to the outcome. Although a series of principles almost amounting to 'Tribunal case law' was established in the 1960s the changing membership of the Tribunal undermined their value. Moreover, even without proving 'monopoly abuse' the Tribunal could vary the Society's tariffs. Perhaps worst of all when inflationary price rises necessitate fairly frequent revisions in tariffs, the Tribunal's hearings add to the delay in negotiating. This may have been one factor contributing to the apparent decline in the real value of distributions to members between 1967 and 1970.

On his appointment as General Manager in 1965 R. F. Whale stated: 'I think the Society has been influenced too much in the past by the belief that the best measure of efficiency is a low expense rate . . . The first priority has to be distributable revenue, not low expenses.' Unable to use 'hard sell' techniques because of the ever present possibility of opposition from music users, the Society was forced to seek alternative means to increase its revenue. These included increases in the Society's field staff and expenditure on propaganda in the form of explanatory booklets. Simultaneously the Society in a period of increasing labour costs has sought to mechanize its collecting and distributing operations by computerization. Despite the acute market problems facing the Society – as Whale said: 'the seaside landlady is a formidable person in the performing right world. . . . The opposition we meet here is out of all proportion to the fees payable'[1] – the Society has been remarkably successful in increasing its revenue, and with the expansion in the composers' market each year has seen an increase in the Society's total revenue. Indeed, reviewing the long-term trend between 1939 and 1970, in only one year, that of the outbreak of war itself, has the Society suffered a fall in its total revenue.

'To exercise and enforce the rights of its members, to restrain unauthorized use of their works, . . . to collect fees for permission to perform the same in public': these were the Society's aims in 1914. In the period since 1939 membership and income have both increased. Despite the pressure from commercial

---

1. This remark was occasioned by the efforts of seaside MP's during the passage of the Copyright Bill 1965 to secure advantages for promoters of seaside entertainment. These efforts were frequently made in the name of the seaside landlady.

interests, anxious to exploit new methods of musical reproduction, the Society has fully protected its members under the
aims laid down in 1914. The composer has been successfully
delivered by the Society from the age of sheet music into the
age of electronic music.

5
The Market for Musical Composition Today

Introduction

In 1911, the principal sole rights granted to the composer were those of reproduction (which was to mean most importantly reproduction in mechanical form), publication and performance in public. Under the Copyright Act of 1956 the public performing right was made distinct from the broadcasting right and that of transmission to subscribers of a diffusion service. These rights are of fundamental importance to the composer in protecting the property which he has created but they tell us nothing about the commercial relationships that must be established if the work is to be exploited. It is the aim of this chapter to examine the relationships which exist in the music market at present between composers, publishers and recording companies. The material on which it is based has been mainly drawn from interviews with music publishers and it reflects their views on the changes at present taking place in the market for musical composition.

The Collection Agencies

As was discussed in Chapter 2, before 1914 the composer approached his market as an individual. He struck an individual bargain with his publisher and the publisher attempted to secure a return for the composer and himself, mainly through the sale of copies of sheet music. In order to equalize the risks and rewards between the composer and the publisher, the royalty system of payment was introduced. The growth in record sales led to a decline in the importance of sheet music sales which the establishment of the public performing and mechanical rights helped to offset. Because of the administrative difficulties and the high transaction costs involved in the performing right, composers and publishers created a specialized agency, the Performing Right Society, to organize and exploit the right. Until 1956 the Society struck its bargains with music users without reference to any other interests, but with the establishment of the Performing Right Tribunal a third element, the public interest in guarding against the possibility of monopoly abuse, has been added to negotiations. In addition to adjudicating on the composer's performing rights, the Tribunal's jurisdiction extends to his broadcasting and diffusion rights.[1] The existence of the Tribunal means that the composer is effectively no longer a free agent when it comes to exploiting his property rights because under modern conditions there is no other way of exercising the public performing right in non-dramatic music than through an agency such as the PRS. This is true also of the mechanical right, where a compulsory statutory royalty was established in 1911 which comes into operation after permission has once been given for a recording to be made. As with the performing right, copyright owners joined together for the purpose of collecting and distributing the revenue from the mechanical right. In this case two societies, the Mechanical Copyright Licences Company Ltd, and the Copyright Protection Society Ltd were formed. In 1924 these two organizations amalgamated to form the Mechanical Copyright Protection Society Ltd. With the performing right, agreed shares of income between the composer, author and publisher were established from

1. But only where they are exercised through a licensing body such as the PRS, and similarly in the case of literary and dramatic works. The Tribunal's jurisdiction also extends, as mentioned earlier, to the public performing right in recordings, whether exercised through a licensing body or otherwise, and to the rebroadcasting right in the broadcasts of the BBC and IBA. It does not extend to the mechanical recording right, which is exercisable in private. None of these rights are in the strictest sense exclusive, since many exceptions are made in the Act in favour of the public interest.

the outset despite the prevailing custom by which composers and authors assigned the whole of their copyright to the publisher.

This was not the case with the mechanical right. Here the whole copyright is assigned, and the basis for mechanical royalty shares depends solely on the bargain struck between the composer and the publisher. Excluding the compulsory royalty provision, the arrangements for the distribution of mechanical royalties retain an important degree of flexibility. This was to be of some significance with the establishment of small recording companies in the 1950s. It was also an important factor in persuading composers to protect their interests by forming societies such as the Composers' Guild and the Songwriters' Guild. Through them a united front could be established and the existing trade conventions surrounding income shares could be influenced. Thus the establishment of standard and 'approved' contracts was one of the earliest tasks of the Guilds. One other difference between the performing right and the mechanical right is also worth noting. In the case of the performing right, the PRS acts as a collecting agency for all publicly performed music. Except in the case of opera music and music for drama, no private bargains are struck between copyright owner and music user. On the other hand, not all mechanical royalties are collected by the MCPS. A large number of copyright owners collect their royalties direct from record companies and thus save the cost of an agent's collecting fee. Unlike both performing and mechanical rights, no collection agency exists in the field of sheet music. Royalties are transmitted directly from the publisher to the composer. The collecting agencies for performing and mechanical royalties were established as a result of the 1911 Copyright Act. The latest collecting society, Phonographic Performance Ltd, was formed after the Carwardine case in 1933 when it was held that the copyright in records included a public performing right. This right was used to limit the public performance of records but where such performance was licensed the owners of the copyright, if any, in the works recorded were granted an *ex gratia* share of PPL's royalties. Such share did not necessarily come back to the original composer or author unless a specific contractual obligation existed. The mechanical recording right collection societies do not, however, act for the composer of specially commissioned film music, where the right to record on the film sound track (commonly called the film synchronization right) is exercised by the composer himself through his commissioning contract. Such then is the broad legal and institutional framework which exists in the composer's market and which forms the essential background to any discussion of the relationship between composers, publishers and recording companies in the market today.

Although serious and popular composers have both experienced a marked increase in the demand for their works over the last twenty years significant differences exist between the two markets which they supply. We consider first the market for pop music and then that for serious music.

Publishers of 'Pop' Music

Before 1914 any discussion of the music market, popular or serious, would have begun with the publisher. It was to the publisher that the composer went in order to find a market for his music. Sheet music sales were the main source of income and the publisher's function was to generate sales by popularizing the work through advertising and concert performances. The publisher also matched lyrics with music and both with the star performers of the day. Most important of all, the publisher bore most of the risk. Although the publishers could still claim in 1928 that publication was vital to the creation of a market, it is clear that the range of activities covered by the word 'publication' had altered considerably. Sheet music revenue was declining in the face of increasing record sales and commercial success depended on much more than concert promotion. The twin props of the publisher's business looked distinctly unreliable and publishers needed to adapt to survive. Their reaction was to increase their agency activities. What they now began to offer the composer was not their knowledge of publishing sheet music but their experience of the music market. In place of sheet music sales they offered to find recording contracts, broadcasting opportunities and commissions for film music. Along with these functions the publisher could also offer an expert knowledge of the collecting agencies. In exchange for these services the composer assigned his copyright to the publisher and shared with him the recording and performance royalties. Until the 1950s this alteration in the publishers' functions was maintained and accentuated by the growing importance of record sales and access to the mass media of radio and television. Although recording companies did sign contracts directly with composers their interest in increasing record sales meant that they concentrated more on improving recording and manufacturing techniques, contracting the most popular artists and on distribution and on publicity rather than on seeking out the raw material: musical composition. It was left to the publisher to present the new material that his composers were prepared to offer at auditions. Similarly, television and radio producers tended to turn to the publisher for new material instead of dealing with the composer directly. To succeed, the publisher needed, as his predecessors before him, to be a fine judge of the public's changing mood and taste.

In securing his niche in the music market the publisher has relied on the composer's lack of knowledge about how to gain entry to the media. Lacking close contacts with programme builders and artists' managers, the composer was not likely to find outlets for his work. The composer too was unlikely to be able to afford to pay for having his music printed and distributed amongst producers and managers, so that even if sheet music sales had declined as a source of income the actual publication of his work remained important. In the 1950s, however, technology presented the composer with an opportunity of gaining access to the market directly. The tape recorder lowered the cost of recording. By writing and recording his own work the composer could keep his copyright exclusive. At the same time as the tape recorder, the small pop groups appeared in the music market. Arising from the youth culture of the early 1960s these groups relied less on outside material and created their own style of music. The result is that the line of distinction between the composer and the group has become blurred. With the easy access to recording facilities, there appeared what have been described as 'instant music publishers'. These publishers persuaded the agents and recording managers of the pop groups that they no longer required the traditional services of a publisher. Instead they offered to the groups the facilities of a small scale recording company. With the proliferation of these small music companies the traditional music publisher encountered considerable pressure in trying to maintain his place in the music market.

Without the recording right, the publisher could be left with the much less valuable publishing right, and in view of the fact that the division of performing fees was laid down by the PRS no compensating adjustment could be made. Faced with competition from these 'instant music publishers', the response of the music publishers has been interesting. As in most businesses under competitive pressure, one response has been to diversify by setting up record companies and by seeking out artists. In this way the publisher has become a promoter of groups as well as of composers. One of the traditional publisher's skills which is still valuable is straightforward administration, and music publishers now perform management services for small music companies. Remuneration is based on either a percentage of gross profits or a shareholding (usually 50 per cent) or a percentage of record sales. The last form of remuneration usually applies where overseas record sales are supervised by the publisher's network of agents. The management function includes exploiting, printing, copyrighting, where under local conditions any formalities are required, and cover versions (i.e. local issues in overseas territories). In other words, the music publisher does everything except own the copyright.

Apart from diversification and offering management services, two other changes have taken place. In the face of competition publishers have accepted a lower price for their services by lowering the royalty share demanded. Whereas contractual terms are virtually standard throughout the industry, an exception is made when the publisher is supplied with a ready-made record and the writer looks for exploitation to secure its success. As the publisher no longer has to meet the cost of a demonstration record a higher royalty is given to the writer. The last, and least healthy response financially, is that some publishers have become 'bankers'. One form of this involves making large advances to untried pop groups in order to secure collection rights. Another involves buying a share in a catalogue to obtain part of the recording and performing royalties. Both forms are deplored by responsible publishers, though for different reasons. 'Advance banking' is disliked because it tends to generate similar demands from other pop groups. 'Share buying' is disapproved of because it does little to help the writer as there is no promotional effort involved and it amounts 'to simply taking the cream off the milk'.

For the artist who is also a writer, the retention in his hands of the mechanical right is an important form of income guarantee. As most publishers point out, 'good copyright will never die, but an artist doesn't last forever'.[1] By keeping the copyright exclusive to himself the artist safeguards himself against the time when the public tires of his personality, even though the music he has created may still be popular. Equally, however, the creation of a good copyright represents the publisher's investment. He hopes for a return over and above that which is necessary to repay the costs of printing, free copies, demonstration records, advertising and distribution so that there exists the strong possibility of a direct clash of interest. One form which this has taken in the United States is a movement amongst groups and composers to *limit* the terms of copyright assigned to the publisher. The aim is either to re-sell the copyright at a

1. Legally, copyright does of course expire, but the distinction the publisher is making is between the popularity of the artist which, given the changing mood of the public, is generally much shorter than the popularity of his music.

higher price if the work is successful or to use the copyright as a form of capital to set up a music company. In both cases there has been resistance from publishers who feel that not only does this make their investment insecure, but that it also means they are morally obliged to go back to composers who assign for the whole life of the copyright and to offer them shorter terms.

While the copyright in a musical work is usually assigned to a publisher for the whole of its life, publishers maintain that they are not led 'to trap' composers into exclusive contracts. On assignment of copyright, the composer is either given an advance payment against royalties covering his potential output for a number of years to come or he is guaranteed a number of recordings. In the latter case a guarantee may be an exceptionally difficult requirement for the publisher to meet if the composer, as is frequently the case, has no prior market success. Where advances are given, publishers point out that it is often they who are 'trapped' and receive no successful songs in return. Whatever the nature of the contract, it is stressed that to be successful the publisher must keep the composer happy: writers who take 'the unhappy pill' are of little use to the publisher because they do not work well and the publisher does not get the flow of composition he wants.

The complaint by composers that publishers take an inordinately long time to review compositions is also discounted by the popular music publishers. Publishers say 'it takes little time to review, but a long time to exploit'. A snap and hurried judgment formed from glancing through a piece of music would hardly satisfy the composer even if it cut the reviewing time. Most publishers emphasize that there is a high degree of personal judgment involved in selecting songs. The publisher feels that in exchange for the copyright he must be able to offer something in return. If the publisher is going to select a song and spend sometimes as long as four or five years in exploiting it he wants to be sure that his judgment is correct. In addition there are delays in the way in which the publisher sets about exploiting the song. The publisher will send the song to the manager of a popular artist to have him try it out. The artist may be abroad on tour and no decision can be made till he returns. Even if the artist likes the tune there may be problems with the lyrics and on top of this it may take six months to record so that a large part of the delays complained about by composers may simply result from genuine attempts to exploit the music.

The popular composers complain that publishers are more interested in promoting groups with their own compositions than the independent composer. This is generally agreed to by publishers. It is however pointed out that this is as much due to the changed nature of the pop market as to the publisher's own inclinations. The publishers have had to take into account that groups normally wish to use their own material and refuse to record outside songs. Now that the primary function of the publisher is to administer the composers' rights and do everything he can to promote them the publisher tries to organize a 'package' deal with a pop group. If a group already has a recording contract with a record company the publisher's job becomes much easier as it cuts out 50 per cent of the package. Record companies now take material from independent record producers instead of only making their own recordings. Publishers agree that it is getting more difficult to interest recording companies in the work of unattached composers.

The publisher today sees his role as that of finding suitable written material and exploiting it through recording contracts and broadcasting performances. If the material has been produced by a pop group then the publisher will normally undertake to exploit the whole of the copyright they have created. Although sheet music now plays a minor part in copyright income, a 'hit' record can still generate subsequent sheet music sales. Despite this however there is no doubt that *publishing* in the old sense of printing sheet music has all but disappeared from the composition market. In what is unanimously described as a 'highly competitive, cut-throat' industry the music publisher has been able to survive the redundancy in his traditional skills in the face of new technology by adapting these skills to suit the changing nature of the market. The new skills he offers are not essential to the success of a record: Benny Hill's song 'The Fastest Milkman in the West' did not have a publisher and it reached a million record sales without one. Benny Hill publicized the song through his own television programme and then sold either a master tape or record direct to a recording company. As it was put to us by one publisher 'this shows good business sense as it saved him giving away 50 per cent to a publisher'.

The possibility of creating a hit through access to the media without relying on the services of the publisher emphasizes both the fragile nature of the publisher's grip on the market and the extreme importance of the media. The interdependence of broadcasting performances and success in the pop record market is probably felt most keenly by the publisher who is trying to get across to 'the air'. As a result, the publisher finds the 'needle-time restriction' promoted by the Musicians' Union very irksome. It is felt that the restriction directly curbs the amount of new material coming forward and that it is to the detriment of British music because the BBC can avoid the restriction by using foreign recordings. Although the adverse impact of records and broadcasting on the employment of musicians in the 1930s is acknowledged by older publishers, both they and the younger publishers argue that the restriction is based on a false assumption about present market conditions. Publishers maintain that if it were relaxed there would be more recording work for musicians and that this would more than compensate for any loss of employment. Although the restriction conflicts with the publishers' interests, some do recognize that the restriction is beneficial to the older musician who has been most affected by the arrival of the pop group. Publishers live in the hope that increase in demand for pop music from the development of commercial radio will lead to a relaxation of the needle-time restriction. The bottleneck in the media at present has created a situation where most records 'never see the light of day'. According to one publisher, 150 singles, i.e. 300 songs, are released each week but 'BBC policy results in only 10 per cent being actually heard'. Records have to be played on the media to have success, as it is no longer possible to promote new artists through live public performances. This means that the 'plugging' problem has become much worse.

Whereas the serious music publishers tend to emphasize the good work being done for serious music by some BBC local radio stations, the pop publishers welcome the advent of commercial radio because it should reduce the influence of the BBC on pop music.[1] At present only Radio One influences the charts and 'the tastes of the BBC producers lead to a lot of music being neglected'. With commercial radio it is hoped that a wider range of music will be popularized. Despite their natural enthusiasm for the further propagation of pop music, a majority of the pop music publishers interviewed are in favour of supporting serious music. It is generally agreed that the promotion of serious music is not only a good thing in itself but could contribute to the musical development of pop music. This 'uncovenanted benefit provided by the serious composer could best be taken care of by adjustment of the royalty payments made by the PRS, i.e. by mutual agreement.[2] Only one pop publisher wanted to see the government subsidize serious music to encourage British writing and investment in British music.

Publishers were asked if they were satisfied with present methods of negotiating performing rights and the charging systems used. Many compliments about the work of the PRS were expressed: 'they do a good job', 'a band of gentlemen, the fairest in the world', 'it does a first class job'. One publisher felt however that the Society was not sufficiently tough in its negotiations with music users. Comparison was made with the German Society GEMA which was felt to be in a stronger position

1. Strictly speaking, the BBC's monopoly of radio broadcasting in the UK was broken when, in 1964, the Postmaster General granted a licence for commercial broadcasting to Manx Radio, but this licence restricts transmissions to a power which limits reception to the Isle of Man only.
2. In fact, the PRS distribution plan has for very many years been weighted in favour of serious music.

because of its control over the mechanical as well as the performing right. This publisher argued that from the music user's point of view, separate bargaining by the PRS and MCPS was inefficient and allowed the user to play one Society off against the other. A joint approach would secure a higher royalty, and also the administrative costs (and the 15 per cent collection charge by MCPS) could be cut if computer facilities, etc. were shared. Other publishers were much less favourably disposed to the idea of amalgamation. It was claimed that although, unlike some other Societies, GEMA has managed to obtain an 8 per cent mechanical royalty, it has had to give concessions and has not been able to obtain an advance on this figure after twenty years of negotiation. It was acknowledged nevertheless that GEMA, unlike other Societies, had been able to promote legislation requiring the makers of recording apparatus likely to be used for the making of unauthorized recordings to make royalty payments to the owners of the copyright, if any, in the works recorded. Also publishers felt that an amalgamation would decrease revenue if it meant that they no longer received their mechanical royalties direct from record companies as they would have to pay a collection fee on the money. Not only do large record companies pay the recording right owner directly but they also pay interest (bank rate plus 2 per cent) on outstanding royalties when they fall behind in their payments. Smaller record companies simply pay a deposit to the MCPS for a concession.

Lastly, publishers were asked what amendments they would like to see in the law of copyright. The main reply to this question brings this study of the music market to 'full circle' for, as in 1911, so in 1972 piracy – this time of records – stands as a major challenge to the value of the protection given by the copyright laws. The 'bootlegged' tape recording and the pirated record pose a serious threat to the commercial basis of the industry. As in 1911, the problem is not so much one of lack of legal protection as one of detecting infringement of copyright.[1]

1. Some countries have now adopted special legislation to combat this piracy (a
    recent estimate put at some 50 per cent the proportion of illicitly made record-

Other areas of difficulty mentioned by publishers were the evasion of royalty payments in the import and export record business, the demand by some composers for a 'reversionary right' clause in contracts where the copyright would revert to the composer if the work was out of print, and the need to increase the statutory $6\frac{1}{4}$ per cent royalty on records. In view of the 1956 Copyright Committee's recommendation that the period of fourteen years prescribed by Section 19(3) of the 1911 Act as the minimum for the revision of the royalty rate for compulsory recordings should be reduced to one of five years, it does seem strange that no attempt has been made to seek a revision which has not, in fact, been made since 1928. A possible explanation lies in the growing number of amalgamations of publishing and recording companies.

Publishers of Serious Music

Six main large firms operate in the field of serious music publishing. Of these, three (Novello, Boosey & Hawkes and Oxford University Press) are British. Although, like popular music publishing, subsidiary rights from the use of music in television, records and cassettes have increased in importance there are some areas where publishing is still limited to sheet music sales. For example, in the educational field there are no outside royalties and all income derives from the sale of sheet music. As well as sheet music publishing, most serious publishers have a rental or hire business which covers symphony, stage, opera and ballet music. Serious music publishers, like publishers of 'pop', wish to obtain recording contracts for their composers but there has not been the same forward integration into record production as in the pop market. The serious publisher still relies on

---

ings circulating round the world) and an International Convention (The Convention for the Protection of Producers of Phonograms against Unauthorized Duplication of their Phonograms) was adopted in 1971 to induce other countries to take similar action. Piracy via satellite broadcasts is a new development against which an International Convention is now (1972–3) under consideration.

obtaining commercial recordings from the record manufacturer.

Although the income from performing and mechanical fees has grown, the serious music publisher is still very much concerned with the level of profitability in sheet music publishing. Serious publishers have been forced to restrict the rise in sheet music prices (a sheet song cost 2s to 2s 6d pre-1939; 3s in 1960, and 6s in 1970) which have not kept pace with the consumer price index. Accordingly, the publisher finds that he cannot pay sufficiently high salaries to attract the necessary skilled staff and that the retail trade has become less interested in stocking sheet music. With increasing publishing costs, commissioning, another traditional form of support for the serious composer, has become less frequent. It is no longer sufficient for the publisher as commissioner simply to pay the writer a fixed sum. A single manuscript score of a symphony may cost between £300 and £400 but then if a full score of orchestral parts is provided the cost rises to around £2,000. With opera, costs are even higher and a figure of £20,000 has been suggested as the cost of producing a full set of parts. As publishers emphasize, it is not just a question of covering direct printing costs but also the overhead costs incurred by having a fully qualified staff to arrange performances and recordings all over the world. Concert music relies very heavily on performance royalties and a large staff is necessary to arrange performances.

Unlike popular music publishing, new forms of musical reproduction have not lowered costs. There is less room in serious music for the exchange of tapes internationally as the need for translations of texts prevents this. It is also limited by the conventional nature of serious music notation. Performers tend to need a conventionally notated score though serious music publishers now have graphic scores and electronic music in tape form only.

The serious publisher still devotes his time to promoting composers rather than groups. The publisher asks a conductor to examine a score with a view to its performance. Although there is less of a 'personality cult' in serious music than in pop, a composer's success may depend very much on who interprets his work. Different attitudes exist among the soloists who play an important part in promoting serious music. Unlike the pop artists who start by asking what a composition 'is going to do for me', the soloist commonly adopts a less self-centred approach. The vetting of compositions for broadcasting purposes is regarded as fair, on the whole.

The division of royalties from serious music is as follows: sheet music royalties vary between 10 per cent and 12 per cent to the composer; the mechanical right is a straight fifty-fifty split, as is generally the performing fee. With opera and stage works, royalties received are split one third to the composer and two thirds to the publisher. In hire fees, the publisher usually takes between 50 per cent and 75 per cent.

Despite the smaller number of firms in serious music publishing, the force of competition is said to be quite strong. As much serious music is out of copyright the degree of competition varies between the copyright catalogue and the more competitive non-copyright catalogue. 'Under-pricing' has been a feature of the latter, with publishers accepting lower profit margins in an effort to increase their share of the market. Serious publishers say they find it increasingly difficult to make a direct profit from sales of non-copyright music.

Within serious music the prevailing fashion for 'in' names means that the serious publisher is almost operating in the same conditions as the pop field. This has altered the economics of the business for it means that the solid support of the publisher, his 'backlist' of old but still popular works which have paid off all their costs, is no longer available to subsidize new (and loss-making) music. Without masterpieces to add to the backlist of 'evergreens', the future of the subsidy for new works looks uncertain. Its disappearance would mean the ending of an important link between composer, publisher, performers and the public, though the impact would depend on the firm involved. Oxford University Press, for example, might still be able to subsidize serious music out of the profits from educational publishing, having no outside shareholders and with any profit going to subsidize academic publishing or to the University. Commercial pressures as a result are less severe on an academic publisher such as o u p than on, say, Boosey & Hawkes where, as a public company, serious music is subject to tight budgetary control. It is felt that most purely commercial serious music publishing firms must have put a lot of money into ventures with a low return. Whilst this helps British music it does mean that the publisher could probably have made a higher rate of return by investing his money at normal interest rates. The short-lived nature of the most successful works and the consequent drying up of the 'self-subsidy' source may well limit further the ability of the publisher to invest in new works in the future. It is likely that the realization of this has been one of the factors which has made publishers less willing to take risks with avant garde music. Most serious publishers feel that, given the limited demand for electronic music, they cannot afford to take risks: 'the nature of the composition is changing, the number of performances is limited, but the amount of composition is not'.

Performance, as in pop music, appears to set the limit to the amount of composition which the market can absorb. The supply of music is described as being 'wildly' in excess of demand and from this follows a number of the less pleasant features of the market for new composers. The large number of manuscripts submitted to publishers inevitably results in extraordinarily long delays, as few publishers can afford to maintain the large specialist staffs to review them. Because of the importance of access to broadcasting, scores are passed on from the publisher to the b b c, where further delay occurs. Even when a publisher favours a score he then has to seek exact costings of its publication and this imposes further delay.

The limited nature of the market for serious music influences the type of contract between composer and publisher. These are of two types: the 'one-off' contract where the composer carries out a particular piece of work for the publisher, and the general contract, 'first refusal' basis. Another factor which limits the number of contracts on offer to composers is the specialized nature of their product, which calls for a special relationship between composer and publisher. Publishers perform an agency function by looking after composers' interests in the widest sense because of the subsidiary rights. The publisher wants to be able to understand what the composer is trying to express through his work and the demanding nature of this kind of relationship means that only a few composers can be offered long-term contracts by any one publisher.

The most pressing problems for serious music publishers associated with the law of copyright are the state of copyright in the United States and photocopying. Photocopying in particular hits the educational composer wholly dependent on sheet royalties. Serious publishers would like to have some form of remuneration based on a levy on photocopying machines akin to that imposed on tape recorders in Germany (see p. 158). They also point out that while the public reaps an immediate benefit from evading the royalty by photocopying, in the long run this will mean that fewer copies will be published and these will be more expensive.

Although most serious music publishers think that some form of subsidy is necessary for serious music they would rather see a greater number of performances 'as this would enable composers to take care of themselves'. Composers, they feel, do not want to be too cushioned and they cannot 'write in a void'. A better flow of income from performance would help to alleviate this. At the moment the varying frequency of performance amongst composers results in an extremely uneven distribution of income with 'the top too well paid . . . and the bottom underpaid'.

All in all, the music publishers have faced a difficult task in trying to retain and to improve their economic position in the teeth of rapid changes in both technical and institutional structure on the supply side of the market and the changing pattern of demand from music users, particularly the broadcasting companies and the overseas market.

Postscript

We stopped the clock at the beginning of the 1970s, but even during the short period between completion and publication of this work three new developments have taken place which are bound to have an appreciable influence on the future economic position of composers.

The first development arises from British membership of the European Economic Community, which means that EEC anti-monopoly legislation will become binding in the UK. We have already seen (Chapter 1) that one of the first cases raised by the EEC authorities concerned the activities of the German agency collecting royalties for performance and mechanical rights (GEMA), some of whose operations were branded by the EEC as restrictive practices. Other collecting agencies within the EEC countries, including the PRS, are now having to consider how far this judgment and the subsequent course of EEC anti-monopoly legislation will affect their plans and to what extent they will be consulted on EEC policy by their national governments.

The second development is the setting up in August 1973 by the Department of Trade and Industry of a new Committee on Copyright Law under the Chairmanship of Mr Justice Whitford. The Committee's terms of reference are wide-ranging and will embrace all aspects of copyright in music. The Committee is not expected to report until the end of 1975.

The third development is the long awaited birth of the first 'legitimate' commercial radio stations. As we have shown in Chapter 5, publishers have welcomed commercial radio, largely because it creates an additional source of demand for music, coupled with the possibility of greater competition between purchasers of music for composers' services. Initial agreements between the PRS and the commercial broadcasting companies over performance royalties appear to have been completed without protracted negotiation.

These developments suggest that the major influences on the market for musical composition in the foreseeable future will be more of an institutional than technical character, though it must be remembered that innovations such as the audio and video cassette make it technically more difficult to trace the amount of 'free listening' to composers' works through such activities as 'home-dubbing' and commercially organized 'piracy' of gramophone records. However, if there is one lesson to be learnt from our historical survey it is that one must be wary of economic forecasting based solely on an extrapolation of institutional and technical change.

Therefore, we are content to sum up by underlining the major theme of this work rather than by advancing some grandiose prediction. The turn of the century saw a situation in which composers entered the market-place relying very largely on their own bargaining skills and the historical evidence suggests that these skills were limited and very unevenly distributed between members of the profession. After almost three-quarters of a century, combined action among themselves and with publishers both to obtain recognition of their property rights and to exploit them has made their position a good deal more secure than it has ever been before. To anyone familiar with the development of other professions over the same period, the move towards collective action stimulated by the growing influence of powerful buyers and potentially adverse technical change does not come as a great surprise. Like authors and artists, they have difficulty in reconciling society's valuation of their services with their own estimate (and those of their friends) of their 'true worth'. But even if it cannot be denied that their material rewards, solely as composers, are fairly meagre alongside those in associated occupations, including those of executant musicians, they owe much to those among their colleagues who have devoted their time to developing the instruments for improving their lot.

We hope that the reader will agree that the story of composers' attempts to carve out a living for themselves offers a fascinating counter-subject to the contemporaneous artistic developments in musical creation in twentieth-century Britain.

Index

Index

Index

Musical boxes 49
Musical composition, characteristics as a 'product' 16–18
Musical Copyright Bill (1930) 71, 75, 78, 86, 130
Musical Copyright Defence Association 44, 52, 88
Musical Defence League 33
Musical Times 53, 57, 58, 60, 65, 67, 68, 72, 94, 96, 101, 105
Musicians Union 41, 70, 71, 75, 76, 92, 93, 101, 110, 113, 116, 118, 119, 134, 156
Myers, R. H. 94, 101, 104

National Anti-Vaccination League 115
National Association of Symphony Orchestras 118
National Chamber of Trade 75
National Operatic and Dramatic Association 75
National Orchestral Union of Professional Musicians 41
'Needle-time' 113, 116, 135, 156
Novello 38, 72, 115, 159

O'Connor, T. P. 34
Opera 24, 30, 41, 73, 100, 101, 108, 159, 160, 161
Orchestras 16, 17, 24, 30, 37, 54, 65, 67, 100, 101, 112, 117, 122, 160
Oxford University Press 72, 159, 161

Panatrope 34
Parry, Sir Hubert 54
Patents, Designs, Copyright and Trade Marks (Emergency) Act (1939) 127
Patti 45
Payne, Walter 79
Peacock, Alan T. 18, 29, 31
Pelling, H. 101
Performing right 23, 36, 44–8, 69–88, 115, 121, 126–46, 147, 148
Performing Right Society Ltd (PRS) 12, 22, 26, 28, 29, 42, 44–8, 54, 69–88, 118, 126–46, 157, 158, 164, 165
Performing Right Tribunal 80, 132, 144–45, 148

Phonographs (*see also* Gramophones *and* Records) 15, 38, 45
Phonographic Performance Ltd 92–3, 116, 133–4, 149
Photocopying 163
Pilkington Committee *see* Report of the Committee on Broadcasting 1960
Piracy 19, 24, 33, 34, 36, 45, 110, 137, 158–9
Plugging 24, 65, 84, 113, 117, 157
Political and Economic Planning (PEP) 61, 97, 107
Poppy 58
Popular music (and composers of) 17, 22–25, 28, 38, 40, 47, 70, 84, 86, 104, 109, 110, 112–17, 121–5, 133, 150–9
Poulsen, Valdemar 102
Public houses 104, 139
Publishers 20, 25, 26, 27, 28, 32–34, 35, 36, 41, 43, 47, 88–91, 93, 103–4, 114, 116, 126, 150–63
Publishing Right (*see also* Sheet music) 36, 40–44, 147
Puccini, Giacomo 30
Punch 76

Queen's Hall 38, 54, 64, 67

Radio 14, 18, 20, 26, 38, 53, 56, 62–69, 81, 94, 95, 97, 101, 106–21, 129
Radio and Television Safeguards Committee 119
Radio Luxembourg 68
Radio Normandie 68
Rank, J. Arthur 113
Records (*see also* Gramophone *and* Phonographs) 14, 16, 19, 25, 26, 42, 51, 57, 101–2, 113, 114, 122, 129, 134, 147, 151, 159
Re-diffusion 68, 85, 97, 129, 147, 148
Reith, Lord 62, 63, 118
Report of the Broadcasting Committee (1926) 66
(1949) 113, 115, 116, 117, 118
Report of the Committee on Broadcasting (1960) 120
(1970) 114

Index